THE
Geography
OF Survival

ECOLOGY IN THE POST-SOVIET ERA

"In recent years the damaging environmental effects of communism in central and eastern Europe have been extensively described. Will post-communism be worse?

"In this new book, Ze'ev Wolfson—who under the name Boris Komarov wrote a classic about the destruction of nature in the Soviet Union—describes the environmental deterioration in the northern and southern parts of Russia. In the weak and fragile ecological conditions of Siberia, production of oil and gas is the driving force behind ongoing decay. In the south, cotton production is one of the damaging factors contributing to both water pollution and shortage. Even after reading many publications about environmental destruction in the former Soviet Union, it is not possible to read these pages about the author's native country without any emotion.

"Perestroika brought more instead of less ecological destruction, with ensuing international and global environmental risks due to the 'eco-domino' effect—the momentum of ongoing processes of ecological deterioration that can hardly be stopped once they have started. The nuclear nightmare has been transmuted into an ecological nightmare.

"The lesson of the book is that we should interpret environmental problems in Russia no longer from the perspective of a society suffering under communist totalitarian state control, but a society in a state of anarchy and suffering from a breakdown of government control. Contemporary Russia is in need of help from the west, but also of protection against the west—among others, against its atomic lobby and chemical waste mafia."

—Egbert Tellegen
University of Amsterdam

Also from M.E. SHARPE

The Destruction of Nature in the Soviet Union
Boris Komarov

Environmental Action in Eastern Europe
Responses to Crisis
Barbara Jancar-Webster, editor

China's Environmental Crisis
An Inquiry into the Limits of National Development
Vaclav Smil

THE
Geography
OF Survival

ECOLOGY IN THE POST-SOVIET ERA

Ze'ev Wolfson
(Boris Komarov)

author of
The Destruction of Nature in the Soviet Union

With a Foreword by
YURII SHCHERBAK

M.E. Sharpe
ARMONK, NEW YORK
LONDON, ENGLAND

Library of Congress Cataloging-in-Publication Data

Komarov, Boris
The geography of survival : ecology in the post-Soviet era / Ze'ev Wolfson.
p. cm.
Includes bibliographical references and index.
ISBN 1-56324-075-0. ISBN 1-56324-076-9 (pbk.)
1. Environmental protection—Former Soviet republics.
2. Former Soviet republics—Environmental conditions.
3. Conservation of natural resources—Former Soviet republics.
I. Title.
GE160.S65K66 1993
363.7′00947—dc20
93-4081
CIP

Printed in the United States of America

The paper used in this publication meets the minimum requirements of
American National Standard for Information Sciences—
Permanence of Paper for Printed Library Materials,
ANSI Z 39.48-1984.

BM (c)   10   9   8   7   6   5   4   3   2   1

BM (p)   10   9   8   7   6   5   4   3   2   1

Contents

List of Maps

List of Tables and Figures

Tables

Figures

Foreword

Speaking to the opening session of the global environmental conference held in Rio de Janeiro in June 1992, UN Secretary General Boutros Boutros-Ghali said that all of Man's victories had been victories *over* Nature. "But," Boutros-Ghali warned, "the world is finite. Nature in the true sense of the word is no more." The idea that a boundary had finally been crossed, and that development of the planet had become increasingly dangerous, was the focus of every presentation at the "Rio–92" summit. What became unmistakably clear in Brazil was the extremity of the situation and the strength of political will that would be required to save the planet.

Ze'ev Wolfson's *Geography of Survival* exemplifies the "spirit of Rio," the spirit of concern and hope, knowledge and foresight. It is not a hastily assembled set of banal statements about fashionable ecological subjects.

Leo Tolstoy once said that a real novel should begin with the protagonists' marriage rather than end with a romantic kiss before their wedding. Basically, Wolfson's book begins where most other ecological publications end. The author goes beyond the simple statement that environmental pollution has no regard for national boundaries and that ecological problems have acquired a global character. He adduces a wealth of factual material to expose the mechanism of the catastrophe, the way in which it is spreading over the planet, and its causes and possible consequences.

The Geography of Survival offers dramatic proof of the way shortsighted political solutions have led to grave environmental damage and in the course of a few decades turned the former USSR into one of the most dangerous places on Earth. Here the author advances what he calls the "eco-domino" principle, analogous to the domino effect Zbigniew Brzezinski described in world politics. Wolfson shows how aridization, loss of natural soil, destruction of fresh water resources, and other ecological problems in one region "push" neighboring regions to the brink of degradation. The dominoes are toppling from East to West—from the Aral Sea for thousands of kilometers toward Europe and from the Kola Peninsula toward Scandinavia. Waves of ecological refugees—for instance, from Karakalpakia on the shrinking Aral Sea and from the area of the Chernobyl Nuclear Power Plant disaster—follow the same westward path.

It is no coincidence that the author focuses his study on two regions of the former Soviet Union—Central Asia and the polar regions. A former Soviet citizen, Wolfson received his training in Moscow University's Department of Geography. As an employee of the Department of Nature Preserves, he was able to travel the USSR far and wide and gather a wealth of data on environmental conditions.

In 1979 Wolfson wrote a daring and sensational book—*The Destruction of Nature in the Soviet Union*—that exposed the ecological crimes of the USSR's communist regime. Initially he hoped to publish the book in Moscow, but that proved impossible, given the determination of the Brezhnev government to suppress all information about the country's deteriorating environment and quality of life. Moreover, the author was already known to the KGB as a Jewish activist. Published in the West under the pseudonym Boris Komarov, *The Destruction of Nature in the Soviet Union* was translated into English, German, Japanese, Italian, and other languages. It aroused great interest and was praised by Aleksandr Solzhenitsyn and Andrei Sakharov as well as environmental experts and activists around the world as the best available source of information about the ecological crisis in the USSR. I recall that my parliamentary colleague Aleksei Yablokov and I discussed the book with then Senator Al Gore (now Vice President of the United States) during his visit to Moscow as a guest of the Environmental Committee of the USSR Supreme Soviet.

And now, fifteen years after the first book, here is *The Geography of Survival*, which shows Wolfson to be a deep, mature, and analytical thinker. The value of the book is not just in its grim diagnosis of a malignant tumor growing on the territory of what was once called the "evil empire." After all, so many scripts for ecological holocausts have been written in the last few years that they have no more power to shock than a vampire movie.

The important thing is that the author outlines the main points of a survival strategy, making good use of the example of Holland, which has a very efficient environmental protection system in place. This makes *The Geography of Survival* an optimistic and constructive work. The reader will find convincing examples of environmental management in the interests of society's stable development. In other words, the message is that all is not lost—yet.

The issues raised by Wolfson in *The Geography of Survival* will be with us well into the twenty-first century, if not beyond. Let us hope that we will use this time to learn the great art of survival, to heed the warnings of scientists, absorb the ideas of planetary ethics, and transcend the concept of development that has brought us to the brink of self-destruction.

Yurii Shcherbak
Ukraine's former Minister of the Environment,
leader of Ukraine's "Green Movement,"
currently Ukraine's Ambassador to Israel

THE
Geography
OF Survival

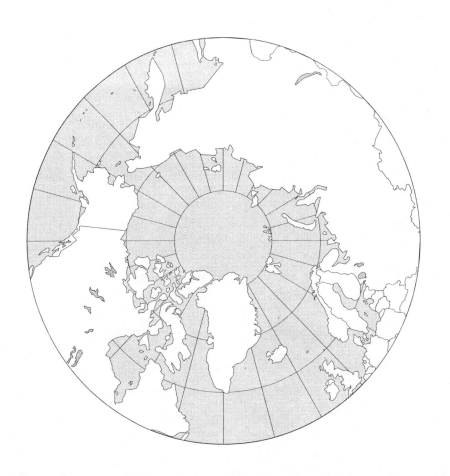

1

The New Geopolitics

Peace has become more dangerous than war—a cruel phrase, yet far from cynical. Our roads are a battlefield, the air is poisoned by toxic wastes, the fields by pesticides, while our oceans have turned into pools of oil. The Third World has been plundered more ruthlessly than the East once was by the Crusaders; no wonder it is now blackmailing us.

—F. Durenmatt, October 1990
(from a speech in honor of Vaclav Havel)

A hundred years ago we knew what was needed to improve life on this earth. We had the answer fifty years ago, when the super-bomb was in the making and we began to live under a constant nuclear threat. Then, about twenty years ago, we awoke to impending disaster—to the prospect of ecological destruction.

The most drastic warning came from Paul R. Ehrlich in his book *The Population Bomb*, published in 1968, which set a deadline—1972—until which time there was still a chance to try to save the earth. After that date, Ehrlich argued, such efforts would be futile: overpopulation and environmental decline would be out of control. The only thing left to do would be "to take care of yourselves and your friends, and to enjoy the little time you have left."

A Soviet scientist named Vinogradov suggested in 1978 that for the USSR the deadline would be 1986 (of course, his report was published "for official use only," and became public knowledge only at the end of 1990).

Earlier warnings of the earth's dire fate had come from American Indians, who were the first to recognize the danger, like an approaching storm sensed from a barely perceptible change in the tint of distant clouds.

Aldous Huxley, in some of his last essays, wrote of what might be called the "death throes" of nature's harmony. Other warnings had come from historian Lynn White (who discovered the original ecological sin in day one of Genesis), Forrester and Meadowes, Masarovich, and the 1972 Stockholm Conference, precursor of the so-called Earth Summit held in Rio in June 1992.

Over the past two decades the frightening forecasts have been multiplying in a geometric progression. More and more conferences, more and more international agreements and standards, more and more people reacting to ecological disasters with growing concern. Does all this attention mean that we need no longer be alarmed about the situation? Undoubtedly there has been progress—real, not imaginary progress—in dealing with some ecological problems. Unfortunately, however, the disaster is not unfolding on paper, with neatly calculated statistics and comforting reports about the success of local clean-up projects. The disaster is unfolding on planet Earth, which has its own system of record keeping.

When I began this book I approached dozens of ecology experts from various countries with a single question: "Name the countries that, in your opinion, do a successful job of protecting their environment." Of course, I had to go into considerable detail to define what I meant by environmental protection. How many recall today that what the experts were worried about in the 1960s was the declining "quality" of the environment—not environmental stability, not simply maintaining an environment suitable for human habitation. By the late 1970s the word "quality" had given way to the notion of "control," or protection. Today it is apparent that this concept is relevant only in wealthy countries, while the rest aim at best for a "safe" environment—one that does not absolutely endanger the life and health of the population.

The majority of the experts I questioned chose the intermediate standard—"control"—with assorted reservations. Now let us project their answers onto the map.

Western Europe: Of the eighteen states (including Luxembourg), fifteen do a more or less successful job of protecting their environment. Spain and Italy rank below them, and Greece does not measure up even to this standard. The total, therefore, is seventeen "positive" states.

Eastern Europe and the Former USSR: None of the countries manage to protect their environment, with the exception of Albania (although even here, industrial development is under way).

Asia: Two countries, Japan and Singapore, are unqualified successes. Another two, South Korea and Israel, do an adequate job, with great reservations. Two countries, Saudi Arabia and Kuwait, have implemented extensive forestation projects, but it is still unclear to what extent they are managing to halt the further advance of desertification. In any case, on the entire continent of Asia no more than six countries may be said to exercise some degree of environmental protection.

America—North, Central, and South: Only in the United States and Canada is there effective ecological control.

Africa: In all of Africa only one country, South Africa (which otherwise rarely triggers positive comments), can be said to deal with environmental protection.

Australia and Oceania: The Australian Union and New Zealand have successful environmental control policies. Australia has grave problems of desertification, but overall the situation can be regarded as stable.

Antarctica: The ecological failures of all countries cause irreparable damage to the natural environment of the sixth continent. Recently, however, there has been a noticeable improvement in the regulations on collective exploitation of Antarctic resources.

To sum up: on the six continents, twenty-nine countries are doing relatively well. These countries comprise 25 percent of the planet's entire area and contain 900–950 million people, less than a fifth of the world's entire population.

The one billion and the four billion. Four billion of the planet's inhabitants would like to attain the living standard enjoyed by the prosperous one billion—a natural and inevitable desire, but what does it mean? In financial terms the answer is simple. The poor countries would have to raise their annual per capita income from $200–$400 to at least $1,500 to reach an American or the European living standard. The language of dollars is universally comprehensible. What is less well understood is that financial prosperity always has an ecological price tag. Ecological price? Some people assume this must refer to increasing numbers of cars polluting the air of large cities, but there is a more immediate price, represented by the correlation between rising incomes and increased per capita water and energy consumption. Better food, intensive industrial production, more comfortable living conditions—all these things entail a correspondingly greater expenditure of water and energy. Indeed, the hunger and poverty of Third World countries are directly related to problems of water production, transportation, and purification. The prosperous one billion residents of Europe or North America consume an average of 4–8 thousand tons of purified water and the energy equivalent of 5–9 tons of oil per capita per year, while for the unprosperous four billion residents of the developing countries the analogous figures are 50–500 tons of water and 0.05–0.7 tons of oil (see figures 1 and 2).

True, these are averages, but I am afraid we will never know the exact numbers. If water and energy consumption in developing countries ever began to approach the American standard, the planet would rapidly run out of areas fit for human habitation (or for gathering data). Every possible source of fresh water, including glaciers, would be depleted once and for all. Environmental pollution and destruction caused by the production, transportation, and combustion of additional billions of tons of oil and coal would create an impact that the atmosphere, the oceans, and the planet itself could never absorb.

This argument is commonly countered by the objection that water can be repurified and recycled. That is true. However,

Figure 1 **Per Capita Energy Consumption, Various Countries**

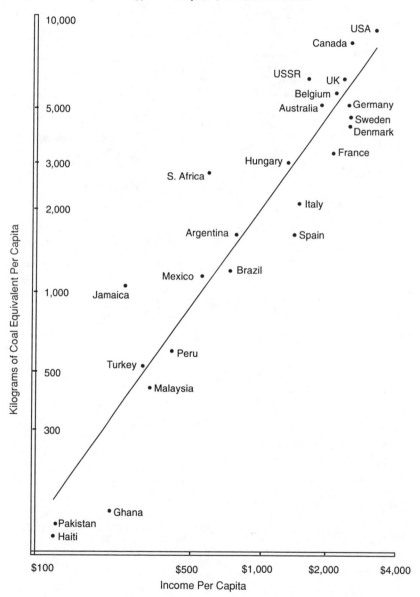

Source: Center for Soviet and East European Research, The Hebrew University, based on various sources.

Figure 2 **Per Capita Water Consumption, Various Countries**

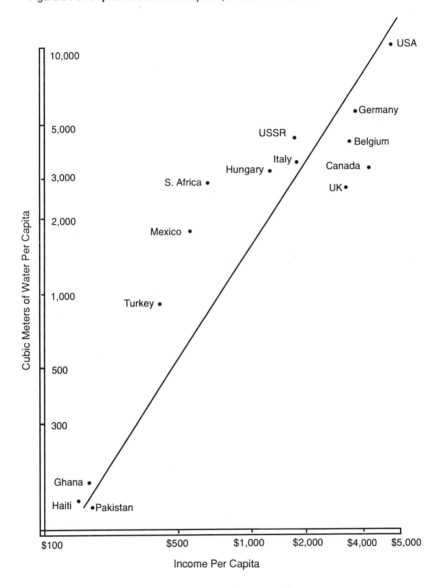

Source: Center for Soviet and East European Research, The Hebrew University, based on various sources.

water purification requires energy, and a great deal of it. The most sophisticated technologies could not close the water cycle fully, as happens in nature; the source of energy must be external, and energy production always means ecological destruction. The extraction of fossil fuels and their burning is inevitably accompanied by environmental pollution. Water purification in one area entails smoke and soot emission in another. Thus, additional supplies of purified water mean additional destruction of the biosphere.

It is also true that the newest technology sharply reduces water and energy expenditure per unit of production, as well as environmental damage. And no doubt, the ever-growing demands that developed countries should share their environmentally friendly technologies with the poor countries are justified. Yet, when this is attempted, it turns out that developing countries are able to assimilate these wonderful technologies only with considerable difficulties, to put it mildly. Three hundred, two hundred, a hundred years ago, Europeans came to America and Africa bringing watches, weapons, and machines that astounded the native inhabitants. Some wise chief may have thought, I do not understand how this works, but my son or grandson will. But modern technology does not accommodate this assumption. By the time the chief's son has mastered a modern, computerized system of irrigation and vegetable growing, that system may be two generations behind the latest technology produced in the United States or Japan. More important, it will lag behind the transformed local conditions of soil and climate as well as the demands of an ever-larger population with a desperately small number of educated "chiefs' sons."

There may be many sound explanations for this state of affairs, but does history listen to reasons or arguments? Will excuses fend off global ecological disaster and the extinction of the planet and of man? Here is what Ehrlich has to say:

> Millions of people are going to starve to death, and soon. There is nothing that can be done to prevent it. They will die because of

short-sighted governmental attitudes. They will die because some religious organizations have blocked attempts over the years to get governmental and United Nations action underway to control human birthrates. They will die because scientists have managed to persuade many influential people that a technological rabbit can always be pulled out of the hat to save mankind at the last moment. They will die because many people, like myself, who recognized the essential role of overpopulation in the increasing woes of Homo sapiens, could not bring themselves to leave the comforts of their daily routine to do something about it. Their blood will be distributed over many hands.[1]

Yes, many are washing their hands—those who have enough water in their water taps. But many more will be left with unwashed skin, with soiled shirt collars circling wrinkled necks. These are the masses, not given to philosophizing, unable to step back and watch as destiny carries out its verdict. The masses have nowhere to go; it is they who will be facing the disaster when it strikes.

Man as a species is destined to survive—in New Zealand and in India, in the Sahara and in the Chernobyl region, in remote backwaters and in the concrete bowels of the metropolis. Man will survive under various conditions. But man as a member of civilized society has much less of a chance.

By its nature, an ecological crisis is longer lasting than a demographic one. After those who lose in the struggle for survival have perished, there will remain the deserts, the soil poisoned with pesticides, the lakes filled with putrefying weeds, the junk and garbage heaps created during the desperate struggle. All of this will remain, and will continue to destroy the natural environment, the impact spreading in ever-expanding circles over the planet.

"Blessed are the Mississippi Negroes who live ecologically virtuous lives precisely because they have nothing—for they will be the ones to save the country."[2] I doubt that anyone today would repeat this statement made by the American biologist

Wayne Davis, and certainly no one who had ever seen the Mississippi, not to mention the Ganges or the Nile, with their hungry throngs, or the televised images of emaciated African children beamed into prosperous Western living rooms. Affluent Americans panic when toxic spray is found on apples, but in Bangladesh, Mexico, Turkmenia, and China the issue is the high percentage of babies born with physical and mental disabilities caused by the huge concentrations of DDT contained in water and in all foodstuffs, including their mothers' milk.

With 20 million residents—up from 9 million only twenty years ago—Mexico City is considered the most populous urban center on earth. It has also been described as the anteroom to an ecological Hiroshima. The city has been struck not by military weapons but by a population bomb. Yet a Mexican delegate told a UN committee that his country would not divert its limited resources for economic development to the solution of ecological problems. Like India and other Third World countries, Mexico is willing to do something for its environment only if Western countries and international organizations pay the bill. "Why do the Americans and the Europeans burn up hundreds of liters of fuel in their cars instead of giving them to us, so that our people could at least cook some food for themselves on kerosene stoves?" the Brazilian representative asked the UN committee. "And after all that they can still demand that our people not cut down the forests for fuel?"[3]

Can the people of the Third World be expected to implement even elementary programs of environmental protection in any conceivable future? In the words of one official in northern India, "We may well be on the way to producing a subhuman kind of race where people do not have enough energy to deal with their problems."

And, perhaps more ominously, can their leaders be expected to resist the temptation to manipulate Western alarm over the greenhouse effect or the depletion of the ozone layer, both of which threaten the "luxurious lifestyle of the rich" first of all? Recall that the Third World press offered virtually no criticism of Saddam Hussein's ecological terrorism when hundreds of thousands of tons of oil were dumped into the Persian Gulf.

Was Ehrlich correct when he singled out overpopulation as the cause of the global ecological crisis? Or should the blame be placed on the combined forces of modern technology and social and national egotism? It does not help to oversimplify the problem: even with low or zero population growth, there is increasing consumption of energy and resources, along with an accumulation of pollution effects and environmental degradation. Blame hardly matters now, for all of these factors are gathering momentum, and the crisis continues its inexorable advance.

One billion and four billion: too great is the gap in living standards, too negligible the chances to narrow it. The West's attitude toward the Third World countries is apologetic in advance. This unease is reflected in the UN report, *Our Common Future*, which argues forcefully that the present trends cannot continue, that they must be reversed, that no country can solve its problems alone, and that unilateral efforts have virtually no chance for success. According to chairperson Gro Brundtland, the UN committee's positive vision of the future, the proposed concept of sustainable development, is based on closer multilateral cooperation and recognition of the growing interdependence of nations.

Our Common Future was the result of unprecedented international cooperation and joint effort in this area, yet the problems remain unsolved. And in fact, the one billion and the four billion will not have a common future. Why not? The simple reason is that the nations of the world have neither a common past nor a common present. It is one thing to draft a plan for international cooperation in protecting the planet, a continent, or a group of countries. But no matter how severe the ecological calamity, it afflicts countries with different political, economic, and environmental structures. The dangers of the greenhouse effect, the rising level of the world ocean, the depletion of the ozone layer—all must be faced by states that are either rich or poor, democratic or totalitarian, North or South, each with its own set of institutions and problem-solving approaches. Each will struggle to soften the blows that threaten it alone, so as to survive as a nation and a society. It is not in human nature to choose equality and commonality in times of crisis and adversity.

The chances for survival will never be "common" or equal for countries and nations with different territories, situated on different continents, at different latitudes, and with different social and ethnic compositions. Distant troubles that pose no immediate threat of reaching their own doorstep will not spur people to action. The cries of millions of victims will be heard stoically by those who are not personally affected. But is this not the line that separates human life from mere survival?

The global struggle for survival brings into conflict not only the First and Third Worlds, for there is also a Second World— the former Soviet bloc states, which until recently remained in the background in discussions of this crisis. In fact they belong in the middle, since in ecological terms they constitute a kind of hybrid between First and Third World countries.

The former Soviet bloc, if for no other reason than its geographic location and its size—17 percent of the earth's surface— plays a critical role in the global ecological situation. Industrial development and modernization may help these countries onto the path of stabilization, improving their own prospects and those of the West, especially Western Europe. But it is also possible— and unfortunately more likely—that development may turn out to be a destabilizing factor that endangers not only their own survival but that of the Western civilization founded on economic prosperity and political freedom.

Let us take a closer look at this Second World.

2

The Northern Front

Seven decades ago the Soviet empire was established on a huge territory, larger than that of any other empire in human history except perhaps its tsarist predecessor. The Soviet Union possessed the richest natural resources in the world—fertile land, forests, fresh water, oil, coal, metals, gold and diamond deposits—everything required for development and prosperity. The boundless expanse of fields, rivers, meadows, and forests stretching all the way to the Urals, beyond which a new expanse opens wide, inspired one with a sense of tranquility, of timelessness, as if history had ground to a stop.

This vastness played an important role in shaping the psychology of the population, the so-called Russian national character, the broad and generous Russian spirit. In the period after 1917 that sense of boundless space and inexhaustible resources became one of the premises of Soviet ideology. It fed the illusion of communism's unlimited potential, its superiority, its ultimate triumph over all other social and political systems. At the same time, Russia's vast territories and boundless skies, its great rivers, lakes, and seas, seemed capable of effortlessly absorbing and dissolving any amount of pollution. They provided a sort of ecological quota, an unparalleled advantage for cheap economic development, and forestalled ecological crisis.

But these illusions evaporated in the early 1980s. In what was more than mere coincidence, both the population's willingness to swallow ideological fictions and the land's capacity to swallow enormous amounts of pollution were simultaneously exhausted. But while the bankruptcy of Soviet ideology has been widely analyzed, the bankruptcy of the land, the scale of the ecological disaster left behind by the crumbling empire, is without precedent in human history, and its consequences have not yet been grasped.

The Soviet output of natural resources accounted for nearly 25 percent of the total world mining output. Whereas the extraction of mineral resources in the world doubles every fifteen years, in the USSR it doubled every eight to ten years.

While extracting about 4 billion tons of energy and other types of resources each year, the USSR produced 12–15 billion tons of solid wastes and pollutants, 164 billion tons (164 cubic kilometers) of polluted water, and over 200 million tons of air pollutants. A significant portion of this staggering amount of waste was waste in a double sense, since it consisted of useful components that contaminated the environment without having passed through any technological cycle, without having been of the slightest benefit to humanity.

Although production of other types of raw materials played a considerable role in the ecological crisis of the USSR, here I will deal specifically with issues related to energy production. One reason for this choice is that the energy production industry is undoubtedly the largest consumer of natural resources and the main source of pollution on the entire planet. But another, crucial reason is the geography of extracting energy resources in Russia. The richest oil and gas deposits are located in Siberia and the North, a region with an extremely unstable and vulnerable natural environment that does not conform to a European's idea of a territory that can be settled and exploited like any other.

We must try to get a clear grasp of the immensity of that part of our planet that we call the North. It encompasses no less than 25 percent of the world's entire land mass (taking the permafrost

Table 1

The Soviet Union's Share of World Reserves and World Production of a Number of Fuels and Raw Materials (in %)

	In world reserves	In world production
Coal	43.0	16.4
Crude Oil	8.8	26
Natural Gas	42.7	43
Diamonds	8.0	29.6
Gold	24.1	21.2
Iron Ore	30.3	25.5
Mercury	11.1	32.3
Phosphate	7.7	25.8
Platinum Group	16.7	48.4

Sources: For figures on oil and gas: *The National Economy of the USSR in 1988* (Moscow), pp. 676–77. The figures for coal have been calculated with the aid of materials from the *Information Handbook, 1984–85* (London: Shell International Petroleum Company, 1985). The figures on supply and production of raw materials cover the years 1980–81 and 1979–80, respectively, and are based on P. Crowson, *Mineral Handbook, 1982–83* (Byfleet: Royal Institute for International Affairs and Macmillan, 1982). See E. Tellegen, "Perestroika and Rational Use of Materials and Energy," *The Environmental Professional* 11, p. 143.

as a basic criterion for defining the North's boundaries). Outside the former Soviet Union, large areas of permafrost are located in the Scandinavian countries and Canada. In the former Soviet Union itself the permafrost amounts to nearly half of the country—its North European part and almost all of Siberia, excepting the southern portion of the Far East. This is 10–11 million square kilometers of land that is highly vulnerable from the standpoint of ecological stability.

The Soviet North, with a population under 9 million, accounted for 42 percent of the entire Soviet output of raw materials in 1980, and for close to 60 percent in 1990.

With a mere 6.7 percent of the world population, the USSR produced 46 percent of the world's entire output of natural gas, 26 percent of oil, a significant portion of coal, timber, mercury, and gold, and so on.[1] It produced 50 percent more energy per capita than the United States; yet the average Soviet citizen consumed only 33 percent of the energy consumed by the average American. What happened to the remaining energy? Part of it was wasted due to outdated, inefficient technology; but that is only a relatively minor part, what could be called the economic component. The major part of extracted energy resources and energy output is literally lost, poured into the ground, spilled into the water, evaporated into the air, contaminating all of them.

Out of the roughly 5.2 million barrels of oil produced in West Siberia daily, at least 100 thousand barrels (some sources put the figure at 200 thousand) end up being spilled into rivers, lakes, the ground. That is why the amount of oil carried into the Arctic Ocean by Siberian rivers exceeds all the oil spilled into the world ocean as a result of accidents with oil tankers and ordinary pollution.[2]

Of the billions of cubic meters of natural gas pumped into the Siberia–Western Europe pipeline, only half actually reaches the Western border. One cubic meter in every two is lost due to leakage or is used to fuel the turbines that pump the gas. Billions of cubic meters of gas are simply burned up by enterprises that either are unable to use it, or are not interested in using it.[3]

From an environmental point of view, the rate at which the Soviet Union wasted resources is more significant than the rate at which it extracted them. No corner of this enormous country is spared from spillage and waste, but the heaviest brunt is borne by Siberia and the North, for the simple reason that they are the richest in energy resources and the most vulnerable ecologically.

The first time I spoke of the calamities plaguing the North was about fifteen years ago. My conclusions were based on my own data as well as the observations of my colleagues at the Institute of Geography of the USSR Academy of Sciences. At that time I was shown the first draft of a classified map illustrating the country's major ecological problems. The map was being prepared by Professor Isakov, for the use of top government officials. On that map, the color red—signifying disaster—marked sites where energy resources were being extracted that had become disaster areas even at the developmental stage, before their facilities were completed. In Siberia and the North, the disastrous red covered an area of approximately 1 million square kilometers. This does not include the pipelines, which, in Isakov's estimation, covered an additional area of 200 thousand square kilometers.

Thirteen years later, when the map had finally been completed and was made available to the public, the total surface of the country's ecological disaster areas was in the vicinity of 4 million square kilometers, out of which 2 million lay in Siberia and the North.[4]

Why are the northern ecological systems so weak and fragile? The first reason has to do with the permafrost. To explain the link between the permafrost and environmental pollution, let me start by relating a documented story having to do with a cemetery situated beyond the Arctic circle, a story that, in our era of global ecological crisis, will sound like a parable.

The cemetery, which adjoined a mining settlement, was located on a hillside—the usual location for cemeteries in the North. What made this case unique was that this cemetery happened to lie on the lee side of the settlement. In this settlement as in any other, coal was used for heating, and the stoves were stoked all year round except for a few weeks' break in the summer. At this point, it is necessary to supply some further information. Moss and lichen are incapable of withstanding the slightest air pollution. In city parks today, the first thing to be checked is the state of the lichens; if they are dying, immediate measures must be taken lest the trees begin to wither as well. However, in the tundra, moss and lichen are all there is. Thus, in the settlement in question, after the moss and lichen had died from the smoke and the dirt that had accumulated on the snow during the long winter, the permafrost layer became exposed and started to thaw. The age-old temperature balance had been disrupted. Now, when the permafrost thaws, unusual things tend to happen; the more solid bodies—stones, for example—are pushed out onto the surface. Of course, the pushing process lasts over a few seasons: the thawing in the summer, the freezing in the winter, again the thawing, and so on. In this case, the most solid bodies happened to be the coffins. The thawing pushed them up to the surface, together with frozen human remains, a sight that greatly disturbed the miners, without, to be sure, turning their thoughts to problems of ecology. The cemetery was moved to another hill and forgotten. By the time the causal chain—coal–pollution–vegetation cover–the thawing of the permafrost—was grasped in all its fatal significance, a couple of decades later, the damage was done. It was too late, not only for the denizens of the cemetery but for the settlement as well.

For accuracy's sake it must be acknowledged that there is more involved here than just the smoke. True, the tundra should not be exposed to heat, but equally true, it should not be driven over with trucks and amphibian vehicles: this traffic destroys the "blanket" of moss and lichen even faster than the smoke does. In short, the tundra should not be excavated for oil, coal, and gas. For the ecological balance to be maintained, 98 percent of the tundra and forest tundra must be kept untouched. While at the middle latitudes, in the countries of Western Europe and in the United States, residential and industrial sites and roads often take up over 40 percent of the available area, with an additional 30–40 percent devoted to agriculture, in the Far North a mere 2 percent is all that can be safely utilized for all purposes. These 2 percent must contain everything: settlements, factories, roads, greenhouses, and deer pastures.[5] A mere 2 percent—yet still an enormous area! Now, why is this the case?

Once again, the geographical and the ecological maps must be joined into one. The ten million square kilometers known as the Soviet North can be roughly divided into two sections. The Arctic part—the tundra and forest tundra—is the more unstable and vulnerable, comprising no less than six million square kilometers. In the taiga region lying to the south (with a total area of 4–4.5 million square kilometers), the same estimates allow for active exploitation of much larger parcels of land—from 10 to 20 percent of the total area.

Two percent of the six million amounts to 120,000 square kilometers, an area far exceeding that of Belgium, the Netherlands, Switzerland, or Austria. If these countries have found their areas sufficient to develop a flourishing economy, the available area should definitely be enough in the case of Russia, since the entire Far North is only a part of the country. Considering the extremely low population density, 2 percent of the area constitutes an enormous potential. The native peoples of the North, whose economy was based on hunting and deer farming, never used the whole quota of 120,000 square kilometers at once.

Well, that is all in the past. The present picture is quite different. The expansion of the mining industry is, of course, far from over; it continues to advance farther and farther north, in an expanding wave of destruction and desertification.

At this point, some readers may harbor the thought that I am exaggerating the seriousness of the situation. They may accept that the northern ecological systems are being destroyed or depleted, yet point out that the same thing is happening in other parts of the world, where the areas being destroyed are far more valuable than the tundra, which is suited for nothing but deer pasturing at best. What makes the Soviet North so valuable? Why do I see its destruction as a crucial factor in the global ecological threat?

To begin with, there is a grave danger, barely discussed until now, that is related to methane and the greenhouse effect. Methane contributes to the greenhouse effect to no less extent than CO_2, which was recently discovered to be the main source of methane evaporation into the atmosphere of the tundra and forest tundra of West Siberia as well as the area of Hudson Bay in Canada. (Until now the main sources of methane have been considered to be garbage dumps, cattle-breeding farms, and rice paddies.) The causes, according to Soviet specialists on atmospheric physics, can be both the exploitation of oil and gas deposits and the melting of the ice layer. In addition, the sand banks of the Kara Sea contain huge deposits of methane in a liquid state. If that area's environment were to undergo significant temperature changes, it would cause methane to be ejected into the atmosphere, which, in the experts' opinion, would trigger great changes in the area's entire chemical makeup. God forbid that we should reach the point of global methane disaster, as Academician Aleksandr Obukhov put it, for then the entire planet will literally run out of air to breathe.[6] The Yamal Peninsula, Russia's northernmost extremity on the shore of the Arctic Ocean, is the land nearest to these dangerous methane deposits. It is also the site of the richest natural gas deposits newly undergoing exploitation.

The Yamal. Of all the types of industrial development, energy production is the most antiecological; of all the areas of the North, the Yamal Peninsula is the most vulnerable. The danger of this combination would be hard to exaggerate. The Yamal is possibly the most vulnerable parcel of land in the world. It would be difficult to find another region, not only within the former USSR but in Canada and Alaska as well, where the ground is as permeated with ice as it is on the Yamal. The ice is covered with a thin layer of soil that can support only moss and lichen.

Deposits of natural gas—a lot of gas—were discovered underneath the ice layer, at the depth of 3.5 kilometers. Two of the bigger deposits alone are estimated to hold 3.5 trillion cubic meters (the world's total annual output is 1.7 trillion). Even with the most careful treatment of the vegetation cover and the permafrost, and the most conscientious attempt to exploit less land than the permissible 2 percent, the jet of gas escaping from the deep boreholes will inevitably be much warmer than their ice walls, and will cause them to melt.[7]

Here is what happened during the drilling of one of the test wells by engineers from the Kara expedition—knowledgeable, experienced specialists, indeed the same people who had discovered the Yamal gas fields fifteen years before. Nevertheless, during one of the drillings natural gas began to erupt to the surface, and accumulated in low-lying areas. The usual practice in such cases is to run as far away as possible, and then ignite the gas by shooting at it with a flare. That is precisely what they did, but the leak proved to be too big. A fire broke out, generating so much heat that within a very short time the derrick sank into the perma-frost layer made up of sheer ice. A blazing geyser rose up in its place. The gas burned as it came up to the surface, but it looked as if the whole tundra was on fire. In order to put down the fire, the original well had to be covered with cement. For that, another well had to be drilled at an angle that gave access to the first shaft. This required a prolonged effort, and the fire continued to burn for months. It was a long time before the burning well was finally "stifled." A large lake was formed in its place. People who come to stand on its shore, though finding it hard to imagine that a fifty-meter-high drilling tower was swallowed whole in its waters, no longer wonder at the smaller lakes recently formed around this area, for fires in the oil and gas fields have become a common occurrence.[8]

The plans for industrial development of the Yamal sparked protests among the ecologists, the Greens, and the local popula-tion itself. The Soviet government would decide to put a hold on projects for gas extraction that had been scheduled before a full ecological examination had been completed, only to turn around and violate its own resolutions. The economy clamors for more and more natural gas to be produced at any price, both for do-mestic needs and for sale to the West. In fact, the Yamal is now subject to full-scale development of the two largest and richest deposits, with a total area of 2,000 square kilometers, and con-struction of communication lines with a total span of 1,500 square kilometers. In addition, a project is under way to build a railway and a gas main with nine, and possibly as many as thir-teen, pipelines reaching from the Yamal to the West.

If the overall percentage of territory being exploited still looks rather unimposing—a "mere" 4 percent—let me stress once again that such figures are often meaningless under the sort of conditions that obtain at Yamal. Here every road, every embank-ment, tips the water balance over an enormous area and contrib-utes to the rapid spread of erosion. What the roads fail to do will be completed by tracked vehicles such as the GAZ–71, the DT–30P, and the "Tiumenets." This last type has been long advertised as an all-purpose, ecologically safe mode of conveyance. In fact, its metal-and-rubber tracks maul the ground more than the other vehicles, while its maximum velocity is little over 10 kilometers per hour. This model may look good on display at a Moscow exhibition, but it is hardly suitable for the tundra. The GAZ–71 is a small tracked vehicle resembling a light tank with a driver's cabin and container in place of the turret. It runs on relatively little petrol—60 liters per 100 kilometers—but leaves a quite noticeable trail in its wake. Today the tundra is crisscrossed by the deep-cutting tracks of this vehicle.

The DT–30P is a veritable monster. It is a diesel tractor, with a loading capacity of 30 tons, capable of floating. Its cabin accommodates up to 5 people; it is capable of pulling a trailer the size of a small house. It burns up to 500 liters of fuel per 100 kilometers. Equipment like this could consume all of the oil produced in the Tiumen region.

For tens of kilometers around the settlements, the ground is split open by vehicle tracks. Helicopters are few, used for top-priority assignments only. Whenever some piece of metal has to be delivered to the nearest drilling site, a tracked vehicle is dispatched. It splashes through small streams, climbs over hills, plows through the marshes. The driver has neither a compass nor a map. How he sets his course, God only knows. He has only one prayer on his lips—that nothing should happen to the vehicle, since he does not carry a shortwave radio either.

Occasionally a vehicle breaks down. Then the driver, together with his passengers, potters about in water and mud, trying to make the repair. Environmental protection is the furthest thing from his mind.[9]

An old vehicle track is almost invariably filled with water, accumulated from rain or the thawing ice. In some places the ice layer is less than half a meter from the surface, and the remaining soil gives the water a yellow taint. As a result, the tracked vehicle has to pick a new route each time, alongside the old road. The thin crust of soil wears off, and a small marsh is formed. The ice layer begins to thaw.

It was these yellow vehicle tracks that first made me give serious thought to the damaging effect of vehicles on the tundra. In late summer the tundra's natural hues reach their maximum brightness: the blue of numberless lakes, rivers, and streams is everywhere edged with the green and crimson of the fast-wilting shrubbery growing in valleys and ravines. Then, from a plane flying over the tundra, one is especially struck by the hideous yellow strips. For thousands upon thousands of kilometers, the surface is crisscrossed with yellow. This yellow invasion reflects more than anything else the problem of stability of the northern ecological system.

"Yamal," writes geographer Iu. Golubchikov, "is actually a mass of enormous ice lumps reaching up to 50 meters (the height of a 16-story building), perched on a sand bank and crusted over by a thin skin of tundra. The Yamal itself rarely exceeds the height of 20 meters above the sea-level." The Holocene occurrence testifies to the fact that the Arctic Ocean is advancing on the coast.[10]

A number of prominent Soviet experts on the North had warned about the danger of the ocean swallowing up large parts of the coastal tundra even before the Yamal began to be exploited, and that applies not only to the Yamal. In many of the coastal areas of the Arctic, chunks of ice slide into the ocean together with their crust of clay, sand, or soil. Sometimes even the trail of a passing track vehicle is enough to slice off another piece of land. That is why the entire land mass does not have to thaw in order for the ocean to capture another kilometer or two of the coastline, to drive another wedge into the remaining land.

It is on these lumps of Yamal ice that hot jets of natural gas will be pumped and a dozen gas lines will be laid; when even a simple vehicle trail causes so much destruction, the effects of such a project can well be imagined.

What will happen to the Yamal, or rather what will be left of it after a few years of intensive exploitation of its natural gas deposits? A chain of small islands and sand banks? Or will the Arctic Ocean not leave even that, just as it left no trace of

Vasiliev Island, Semenov Island, and other areas that have disappeared, probably as a result of melting ice foundations?

The Yamal represents only an extreme example of the catastrophic fragility of northern ecological systems. From the Kola Peninsula to Chukotka there are other huge areas of tundra, forest tundra, and northern taiga subjected to various types of impact. What will be their future?

An analysis of studies by Golubchikov and other Soviet and Western specialists discloses some invariable regularities in the headlong destruction of northern areas. It can be stated that all northern ecological systems (tundra, forest tundra, and northern taiga) are extremely unstable by definition. The reasons for this are many.

First, there are historical reasons. All northern ecological systems were formed under highly unfavorable conditions; their survival is totally dependent on the utmost utilization of photosynthesis and other biological processes. For these brittle systems, the slightest change in environmental conditions may be the equivalent of the straw that broke the camel's back.

The *second* reason is the structural primitiveness (monodominance) of these ecological systems. There is a well-known rule that the simpler an ecological system, the more unstable it is. The North provides an ideal illustration of this rule. Many years ago, Academician A. Takhtadzian demonstrated that the evolutionary progress of flowering plants was assured precisely by their ability to form complex ecosystems, with two to three layers of vegetation cover. Such systems are less easy to destroy or destabilize, even if the ground layer is made up of lichens.[11]

In an area with a number of systems and subsystems and a variety of species, the environmental impact affects a multitude of factors, and the probability that some of them are interchangeable increases, with a corresponding increase in the chances for regaining a stable balance.

By and large, in the North the conditions are simple—and meager. If air pollution causes one type of lichen to wither on the cemetery ground, there is no other plant to replace it, for other types of lichen are just as sensitive to smoke. With the disappearance of one species of plant, the entire vegetation layer is lost; with the disappearance of one layer, the entire structure becomes totally unstable.

The rare parcels of the so-called spotted-medallion tundra have a wider variety of plants, including flowers, which are indeed more stable.* Here human influence is clear-cut, leading to a simplification of more or less complex ecosystems. Forest tundra is replaced by the tundra; the more varied tundra is replaced by its most primitive versions, and later by polar desert. From the simple to the simpler, then to the primitive, and then? Then—collapse.

The *third* reason is the extremely low level of productivity. If in middle latitudes a hectare of forest yields an annual average of 100 tons of biomass, for a hectare of tundra the average output is about 3 tons; for the polar desert the number drops to 0.3 ton. While both averages—3 tons and 0.3 ton—are equally negligible, from the point of view of an ecosystem's loss of stability a transition from tundra to desert is probably as dramatic as the cutting down of the Amazon rainforest to make way for cattle pastures.[12]

Extinction of the vegetation cover causes the permafrost to melt. And the melting of the permafrost literally knocks the ground—and the future—from under every northern ecosystem.

The disappearance of the vegetation means the loss not simply of brush and lichen but of the only carriers of free energy that are capable of stabilizing the northern lands and uniting in a protective shield against the cold, the chaos, the entropy. That is why the disappearance of these pitiful lichen means an infinitely larger loss—the loss of hope. Polar desert gradually transforms the tundra into something akin to its own image, turning it into a hilly, eroded, frozen waste of lifeless small lakes, marshland, and

---

*The same can be said for parts of forest tundra and taiga, which also include a number of tree and brush varieties. Variety also increases the degree of stability since some types of plants enjoy the humid periods while others prefer the dry.

chaos. In the areas where the ice is covered with a layer of sand, the tundra does not turn into swamp; instead, the land stripped of vegetation is covered with dunes and sandhills resembling those in Central Asia.[13]

The most dramatic feature in the whole picture of the ecological crisis plaguing the North is the border interaction between the already ravaged areas and those that have kept their stability and productivity. What happens between these two zones?

A blueprint of that interaction can be seen in the case of the cemetery with which we began. There, the icemelt and the erosion gradually spread sideways, mainly down the hill. The people, of course, were primarily concerned with the cemetery itself, with the thawed-out, erupting coffins; but the icemelt and the erosion were not limited to the cemetery. In the summer, the bared and eroded site of the former cemetery was filled with excess moisture, which seeped out or trickled through to the adjoining, still "normal" lands, moving tens of meters.

The water was changing the permafrost regime; the ice began to "float," causing erosion—that is, cave-ins, gullies, washouts of the soil, and so on—while the lowest-lying areas turned to swamp. Moreover, in the spring this formerly "normal" ecosystem also accumulated excess ice. Melting ice consumes extra energy; this caused a delay in the warming of the soil and the air inside it, which shortened the plants' already brief vegetation period, and thus decreased their yield even further.

The unique feature of plant and animal life in the North is the slowed tempo of growth of all creative processes, while the destructive processes often advance at nothing short of a phenomenal rate. A gully formed in the tracks of a heavy vehicle that destroyed the lichen cover may spread at the rate of 10–15 centimeters a day, or 6–9 meters in one season (the summer season in the tundra amounts to 70–75 days). The advance of the mud-yellow color gradually "devouring" the modest, unbroken green of the tundra can literally be observed with a naked eye, provided the observer remains in the same spot for at least two to three weeks.[14]

Sometimes the combined effect of various factors on an entire landscape accumulates over a number of years. Thus, for example, in the northern taiga, in the area of the Norilsk mines, which produce polymetal ore, heavy metals pollution had no tangible effects on the adjoining valleys for six or seven years; but then, due to an unusually hot summer, entire square kilometers of land began to dry up and deteriorate.

As the *ecological disaster area* (EDA) expands, its influence on the neighboring systems can only grow. This process almost invariably advances, in that sense resembling the *domino effect*. Numerous factors—topography, soil characteristics, and so forth—determine the rate of this ecological domino process, its scale and growth potential. However, I discern the following common regularity: the intensity of the *eco-domino process* is in direct proportion to the area that has already collapsed (EDA), and in an inverse proportion to the degree of deterioration of the EDA. As an indicator of the degree of deterioration, we can take the index of the EDA's decreasing biological yield as compared to the area's average biological yield prior to deterioration. For example, an index of 0.1 means a 10 percent drop in biological yield, if the yield prior to deterioration is taken as 100 percent. I shall attempt to point out the basic components of this eco-domino process, since in the chapters to follow this will be a key concept in the geography of survival.

The ways a deteriorated area influences an adjoining, still stable area include: (a) a change in the groundwater table (in the North this means a rising level); (b) considerable erosion (or salination) of the soil; (c) a sharp drop in biological productivity, and the disappearance of various plant and animal species, which leads to primitivization of all structures; (d) shifts in the physical condition of the environment (climatic changes).

The new ecosystems are distinguished from the previous ones not only by their lower productivity and more primitive structure but also by the reduction of economic and social potential to the level of zero economic growth. Since the ecosystems are unable to reproduce themselves, the reproduction of a native human

30

Map 1 **Ecological Disaster Areas in the Former USSR**

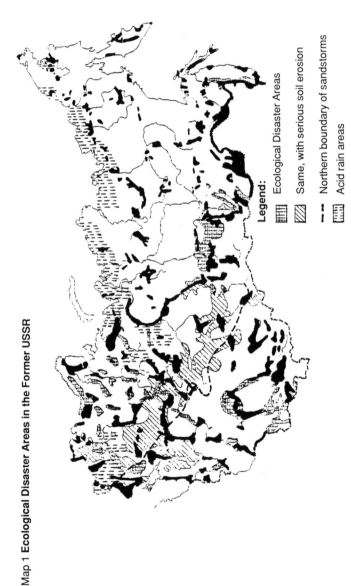

Legend:

▦ Ecological Disaster Areas

▨ Same, with serious soil erosion

–·–· Northern boundary of sandstorms

▥ Acid rain areas

Sources: B. Kochurov et al., "Osnovnoe soderzhanie karty ostrykh ekologicheskikh situatsii," *Prirodno-ekologicheskie sistemy* (Moscow: Moscow Section of the Geographical Society, 1989), pp. 30–41; "Karta naibolee ostrykh ekologicheskikh situatsii," in V. Kotliakov, "Znaky bedy," *Smena*, 1989, no. 12, pp. 74–75; "Karta naibolee ostrykh ekologicheskikh situatsii," in Interview with B. Kochurov, *Iunyi Naturalist*, 1990, no. 4, p. 3.

population and the continuation of their ethnic and cultural traditions becomes doubtful.

I have compared this process of the collapse of ecosystems to the falling of a row of dominoes. The domino theory was popular among political scientists a few decades ago. The interrelationship of geographical and geopolitical factors was indeed of great importance in the creation of the communist and fascist empires, although they were not as crucial as the protagonists of the "domino" theory maintained.

The eco-domino acquires a geopolitical significance since it has a long-distance effect. The problem of acid rain shows that we have already moved beyond the era of localized and relatively simple environmental problems. What used to be a merely local incident now affects large areas, even a number of nations, through water or air flow. What once was viewed as a short-term increase in the level of pollution turns out to cause irreparable damage lingering for generations to come. The eco-domino effect embraces a few types of deterioration; when it envelops large territories, it develops its own momentum (dynamics), which accelerates its further advance. Distance has ceased to be a natural barrier. Thus, a sufficiently stable area located in Europe may be threatened by an eco-domino process triggered thousands of kilometers away—for instance, in the Yamal region.

The actual mechanism of an ecosystem's deterioration is, of course, much more complex than headlong expansion. Only in theory can we envisage a situation in which a vast deteriorated system confronts a totally intact, virginal ecosystem. In practice, both the expanding system and its "victim" are influenced by a variety of factors of pollution or physical destruction of environmental structures.

In addition to the impact of deteriorated areas on "normal" ones, there is also the impact of air pollution, as well as that of various vehicles. Take our old example of the settlement cemetery. Over a period of fifteen years, gullies, land "sores," and marshes spread as far as twenty square kilometers around the settlement, though the settlement itself covered less than one square kilometer. That is precisely what happens in the overwhelming majority of cases.

The biggest and "purest" instance in history of an attempt to industrialize the tundra ecosystems was Stalin's infamous "road of the dead." In the early 1950s Stalin deemed it necessary to construct an alternate route linking Siberia and the Far East, as a precaution against war and possible loss of the Trans-Siberian Railway. To achieve that objective, work began on a new railway line that would run from Vorkuta to Magadan.

By the time of Stalin's death, the section from Salekhard to Norilsk had been almost completed. For 300–400 meters on both sides of the railway embankment, all vegetation—including, most importantly, all the trees—was destroyed. This, together with the railway embankment itself, contributed to a drastic disruption of the soil's temperature balance. Gullies formed, and the thawing of subterranean ice began. Over the next fifteen years, gullies, waterholes, and newly formed lakes swallowed up railway tracks and even whole station buildings. In those years the railway was built by political prisoners, of course, and hundreds of thousands of them perished from hunger and the hardships of slave labor. The railway turned more than a thousand square kilometers of tundra and sparse forest into swamp, desert, and eroded wasteland. To this day no one has reckoned the number of victims claimed by the railway, and almost no inquiry has been made as to the ecological damage it has caused.

Stalin's death put a stop to the railroad construction. With the depletion of coal deposits, coal production dwindled to less than half, many workers left, and the settlements' impact on the environment was considerably reduced. Sooner or later, nature itself reestablishes the balance between the collapsed systems and the more or less stable ones. The loss of another one or two thousand square kilometers was a mere drop compared to the North's expanses. To this day Russians widely believe that Siberia and the North are simply indestructible because of their gigantic dimensions. Thus, when in the early 1970s Solzhenitsyn called for a large-scale effort to populate and reclaim northwestern Siberia, he was giving expression to a belief still preserved among the Russians: that the country has vast places, bigger than any Western country, where one can go and start from scratch, in an environment at once ruthless and rich in natural resources.

According to my data, by the early 1980s about one million square kilometers of tundra were turned into desert and swamp, and up to 0.7 million square kilometers of forest tundra transformed into tundra and swampland. Updated Soviet statistics (finally declassified) indicate that the numbers are 0.9 million square kilometers for the tundra, and the same for forest tundra and taiga.[15]

On the Yamal, even prior to large-scale industrial development, an area of approximately 100 thousand square kilometers was estimated to include 400–500 single sources of impact alone (250–300 test wells, about 150 settlements of various kinds, plus a few thousand kilometers of roads). In "older" areas of development the number of such sources is much greater. Thus, in West Siberia, whose area is immeasurably greater than that of the Yamal (about 1.2 million square kilometers), the number of single sources of pollution reaches 10,000.

Here, as well as in some parts of the Kola Peninsula, in the area of Salekhard, Norilsk, and Yamal, in the Tiumen and Magadan regions, and on the Chukotka, such centers have condensed into knots. There, distances between sources of impact do not exceed 30–40 kilometers. In other areas, framework centers have been formed, with the average distance between them—the EDA borders—about 120–150 kilometers. Obviously, the formation of such centers actually encourages the expansion of EDAs and the increase in the scale of the eco-domino process.

The power of each separate source is correspondingly redoubled. In the near future, the rate of their growth is unlikely to taper off. In the fall of 1990, after a year of wavering and debates, the Soviet government decided to proceed with the construction of five gigantic oil and chemical plants in the Tiumen region at an estimated total cost of 40–100 billion rubles.[16]

The influence of the various types of such centers has already led to the formation of a large number of EDAs ranging in size from 600 to 1.6 million square kilometers. According to Soviet specialists, in 1989 there were 33 such areas in Siberia, and 133 in the entire North.[17] Soviet officials admitted that, yes, 1.8–1.9 million square kilometers is a large area, but compared to the entire area of Siberia and the North is it still less than 20 percent.

Not long ago, in historical perspective, the forest bordered much closer to the shores of the Arctic Ocean. Larches, pines, and birches grew there at an almost regular density. The settlement of tundra, which began roughly ten thousand years ago, would have been impossible without an energy base that could only be supplied by timber. By destroying the forest, however, man undermined the foundation of his own progress. (Could it be for that reason that three thousand years ago on the Chukotka the Bronze Age gave way to another stone age that lasted until as late the seventeenth century?)

The forest line is rapidly receding south, and the strip of tundra that replaced sparse forest has now occupied an area of 0.9 million square kilometers. By my estimates, less than half (about 40 percent) of these forests were destroyed by the local population during the last ten thousand years; the greater portion (60 percent) was wiped out by the last thirty years of industrial expansion.

"Man-made frozen deserts and semideserts are devouring the tundra from the north, while the tundra he has made is pushing at the forest from the south," writes an expert on the North, Dr. Golubchikov. "Only a small share of the transformed surface is taken up by construction sites and transportation lines. All the rest has been ruthlessly poisoned, gutted, despoiled, burnt, destroyed, smeared with oil and grease. Many areas of economic development are surrounded by the by-products of their industrial activity—tundra, deserted badlands, swamps, and sand. The North is moving south."[18] The deteriorated areas are being "northernized" in their climate as well as in the reduction of their vitality.

But where are the greenhouse effect and the increase in global temperature? What about the predictions that the tundra will be covered with forest all the way to the Arctic Ocean, whose ice will almost entirely melt? Are there no visible signs of this in the North? There are. In the tundra, some flower plants have been found that had never grown this far north. Temperatures are rising. But this may affect the melting rate of the permafrost, in which case not only the Soviet tundra but 25 percent of world's entire land surface may be threatened. For the higher temperatures to cause the forest to move north would require thousands of years—which the North does not have. Here the time factor is of overriding importance.

A survey of forestry maps would show that as the area of deforestation widens, the process becomes increasingly self-perpetuating. The collapsed "bald patch" with a span of tens of square kilometers merges with the adjoining collapsed area, then with a third, all of them forming a body that continues to expand at an ever-growing rate. By now the eco-domino process is taking place on a greater, regional scale, where, in addition to the size of the collapsed area and the degree of its deterioration, a crucial role is played by the impact of various industrial and other installations—their intensity, the duration of their effect, their location.

The forest boundary, receding under the influence of the eco-domino process, is what binds together all of the developments taking place throughout the North—on the Kola Peninsula, the Vorkuta and the Yamal, the Kolyma and the Chukotka; even in Buriatia, in the Lake Baikal basin, where sand deserts are emerging to replace the taiga. It can be said that the belt of forests and taiga stretching from west to east, from central Russia to the Okhotsk Sea, makes up that force which has been, and continues to be, responsible for stabilizing the highly unbalanced and vulnerable northern ecosystems. It is these forests, spanning the entire Eurasian continent, that have until now served as a buffer zone against the spread of polar frost and desolation further north. That is why at present, with this mighty forest belt shrinking from both the north and the south as a result of massive felling, with its thinning and breaking down into little islands, what is disintegrating is probably the mightiest stabilizer on the entire continent.

That is why Siberia is Eurasia's future.

And that is why Siberia, a huge natural storehouse of reserves vital to mankind's future progress, represents a danger zone for the entire continent.

3

The Southern Front, or
The Emergence of an Asian Sahara

> All the rivers run into the sea;
> yet the sea is not full . . .
>
> —Ecclesiastes, 1:7

All rivers run into the sea, and the area from which the water flows into the river is called a basin. Once, this simple fact had a merely academic importance, remaining the exclusive domain of professionals—geographers, hydrologists, ethnographers. Nowadays, however, contaminated substances flow down rivers, along with the water. There are effluents streaming directly down the river or washed down from the soil, and particles deposited from the air. Everything flows downward, and, naturally, the larger the area of the water basin, the higher the content of pollution, and the lower downstream it is situated, the higher the concentration of pollutants. There is a high quantity of toxic residues in fish populating these rivers, in vegetables grown on their banks, and in milk from cows grazing in the polluted meadows. Those living in the lower part of the large basins of the bigger rivers and on lake shores are becoming increasingly concerned over the drawbacks of their location. The law of gravity becomes ever more the law of earth pollution.

This is a predicament that spans the globe—from the American Great Lakes to Lake Geneva, the Aral Sea and Lake Baikal, Lake Suva in Japan and Lake Tanganyika in Africa. The Dutch living on the lower reaches of the Rhine and the Meuse basins are compelled to protect themselves from pollution and salination originating in countries situated upstream. Fortunately, the Rhine and the Meuse do not flow into a lake but into the North Sea, which is open and linked to the ocean by numerous currents. Thus, this sea's pollution can be dissolved in the water of the ocean. However, the inland seas, which are largely isolated from the ocean, already contain millions of tons of waste, and are being covered with algae; these include the Baltic, the Black Sea, and the Adriatic.

Most ecological disasters happen due to incompetence and the inability to forecast and evaluate the consequences of industrial and urban development.

The disaster that struck the Aral Sea differs from other similar disasters in one respect: it was planned and carried out deliberately. Central Asia, the heart of the Asian continent, contains one of the world's largest closed water basins, not linked to the world ocean. Two large rivers, the Amu-Darya and the Syr-Darya, carry their water to the Aral Sea. All rivers run to the sea, but the Amu-Darya and the Syr-Darya reach only the lower part of the basin and no further, as it is fully used for irrigation. Since the early 1960s, the level of the Aral Sea has been falling. Today its area as marked on the geographical map should be reduced by 48 percent, for 30,000 kilometers of the former seabed is now a flat surface covered with sand and salt. The photos of rusting ships that were published in the pages of *Time* and *Newsweek* became a haunting image for many people around the world.

The Aral was sacrificed for the sake of cotton—or, as it was said, "for the cotton independence of the Soviet Union." Cotton has drained the Aral. In recent years this explanation appeared in Soviet and Western studies devoted to the Aral. Indeed, cotton does drain two-thirds of the 90 cubic kilometers of water used in irrigation. At some point the Soviet planners figured that if the profit brought by one cubic meter of Aral water (fishing and transportation) was X, the profit from one cubic meter used for cotton irrigation would be X + Y. What could be simpler?

Against the background of Central Asia's flourishing economy, the Aral's role was "to die a beautiful death." This phrase has been attributed to a senior official who was for many years in charge of the country's water management. Even if he never said it, the story has a basis in reality. For seventy years the authorities determined and decided what was necessary and what was superfluous in the natural environment of the country.

The results speak for themselves: about 30,000 square kilometers of the Aral seabed are sand and salt, saline pools, and salt marshes. With 48 percent of the bottom dried up, strong winds (coming mainly from the north on a completely flat path all the way from the Arctic Ocean) lift up approximately 200,000 tons of sand and salt each day. The heavier salt particles settle within the radius of 400–500 kilometers while the lighter salt particles are carried to much greater distances. Salt and fine sand reach the Caspian Sea; the vertical current of evaporation from the water surface raises them to high altitudes, from which they can be carried for ten thousand kilometers and more.[1] In the estimation of physicists in Kazakhstan, the Aral sea bottom produces 5 percent of all aerosols in the earth's atmosphere. Aral salts fall with the rain in Latvia, Belorussia, and Poland. They form layers of dust and salt over the icecaps of the Pamirs and Tyan Shan, which feed the two largest rivers of Central Asia. This speeds up the melting of the ice, somewhat raising the water level in the Syr-Darya and the Amu-Darya, but only for the time being. When the many-meters-thick and many-ages-old ice mass has melted, the irreplaceable mechanism regulating the river flow will disappear, probably for good. The water supply will decrease sharply, especially during the critical summer season.

Is Cotton to Blame? Cotton, which demands more fertilizers and pesticides than other cultures, has played and continues to play a sinister role in the process of chemical environmental pollution of the Aral basin. The sensational data on the rate of infant mortality in the cotton-producing republics, especially in

Karakalpakia, unavoidably point to the "cotton monoculture" as one of the roots of the problem.

A considerable number of villages in Turkmenia draw their water directly from the Kara-Kum Canal. In 60 to 96 percent of all samples taken from the canal, the amount of bacteria and pesticides was much higher than the permitted level. Minister of Health Chagylov explained that the canal receives sewage from cattle farms bordering on the canal, in violation of regulations; residential wastes from the adjoining settlements; and irrigation water containing toxic chemicals. According to the local press, a similar situation can be observed along the Syr-Darya, the Amu-Darya, and some of Tajikistans's smaller rivers.[2]

Here are the findings of the official reports on the content of toxic residues in samples taken in the Syr-Darya and the Amu-Darya from their upper reaches to the delta. At its source in the Pamir Mountains, the water is pure. In the samples taken in the middle, and especially the lower reaches of the two rivers, there is a progressive increase in the content of poisonous substances, including such long-prohibited chemicals as DDT and hexachlorine. Dr. A. Kuzin summarized the test findings as "a deadly dose." The writer Vasilii Seliunin, describing this scene, wrote that Kuzin was pale with fear as he added that "This water is being drunk; there is no other water."

Poisonous chemicals, lethally dangerous in themselves, also neutralize the self-purifying potential of residential and fecal wastes. This repulsive mixture seeps into the water wells. As one expert delicately put it, people are drinking the water someone else has drunk a few days earlier.[3]

The authorities drill wells for the local population wherever they find sources of pure ground water. However, these sources are dwindling, since all surface water in the Aral basin has been badly contaminated. Only 15 to 40 percent of the kind of fertilizers that are used here can be absorbed by cotton plants. The remaining chemicals are washed out of the topsoil and carried into the canals and groundwater. Since this has gone on for many years, it is hardly surprising that dozens of pesticides,

Table 2

Pesticide Levels in Human Milk (in mg/kg)

Country	Area	Year	p.p.DDT	p.p.DDE	-HCH
Belgium	Brussels	1982	0.13	1.0	0.20
Germany	Hanau	1981	0.28	1.2	0.30
Japan	Osaka	1980/81	0.21	1.8	2.3
Sweden	Uppsala	1982	0.10	0.96	0.09
China	Beijing	1982	1.8	4.4	6.7
India	Ahmedabed	1982	1.2	5.4	4.7
Mexico	Morelia	1981	0.82	5.4	0.49
USSR	Ashkhabad	1987	2.2	4.9	6.0

Source: UNEP/WHO reports; Environmental Board of Supreme Soviet, 1989 report.

including DDT, nitrate compounds, and other chemicals, per-meate the environment in virtually every area of Central Asia. They have contaminated the water, the soil, the food, and often the air. Workers engaged in harvesting and cleaning cotton come into contact with toxic substances that damage the body not only through the lungs but through the skin as well. Dis-solved toxins get into food products. In the Chikment region, as tests have shown, the percentage of pesticides found in meat exceeds the safety norm by eight times, and in vegetables and fruit by sixteen times. The nitrates have been dismissed as a mere trifle unworthy of consideration.

In Karakalpakia, pesticides have been discovered in many women's milk in such concentration that doctors have advised them against breast-feeding. But what is to be done when even factory-made baby food occasionally contains toxic residues? For decades DDT has been used to treat cotton diseases, and quantities of it have accumulated in the soil and the rivers. Soil samples taken in the Andijan region in 1989 contained DDT in quantities of up to 2,400 times the permissible level![4]

Objective data testify to the fact that the health of the popula-tion of the Aral basin is approaching the critical point; all the doctors can do is register the events. In Karakalpakia, the incidence of paratyphoid fever is double that of Uzbekistan and twenty-three times the average for the whole former Soviet Union. Over the last ten years, the overall mortality rate in that small autonomous republic has risen by 50 percent. Cardiovascular diseases have increased by 60 percent, gallstones by 500 percent, and stomach cancer by 700–1,000 percent. There have been 60,000 registered cases of jaundice; the victims, doctors believe, will be disabled for the rest of their lives, due to liver damage. Dysentery is rampant in the Aral area; diseases long forgotten by the civilized world have become a common occurrence. The infant mortality rate is higher here than in Paraguay, and twenty times that of Japan, for example.[5]

In April 1990, *Moscow News* featured a photo of a Turkmenian child who was dying (and later did die) of muscular dystrophy, despite medical treatment. The pediatricians admitted that they had never encountered this disease in such an extreme form, not even during the famine of World War II.[6]

Medical examinations given to young conscripts provide an important indicator of the state of public health, for they involve practically 100 percent of all young men. This explains the alarm occasioned by reports issued a few years ago (and unconfirmed by the authorities) stating that 40 percent of all young men in Uzbekistan were found unfit for military duty because of their physical or mental condition. The late Andrei Sakharov, speaking at a session of the Supreme Soviet in June 1989, claimed the current figure had topped 50 percent.

The female half of the population fares no better than the male, but since 18-year-old girls are not subjected to general health examinations, accurate data are unavailable. However, the existing partial figures are a shocking revelation even to those inured to the local conditions: "95 percent of all expectant mothers coming from Tajik villages are unwell or gravely ill. This is a frightening figure, but I want you to hear it and to feel it," said Dr. S. Khakimova, head of the Institute of Maternity and Infancy in Dushanbe. "They should not be allowed to have children at all!"[7]

Pediatricians sent from central Russia to assist their Kara-kalpak colleagues were shocked not only by the disastrous state of the hospitals but also by the tired and sluggish way in which local women reacted to the death of their babies. "This is not indifference," wrote Dr. Terskii, one of the pediatricians. "These women are simply exhausted and gravely ill themselves."[8]

Soviet specialists blame pollution as a key factor in this tragic situation. The main source of pollution is found to be pesticides. The ecologist Yablokov, citing a number of Western and Soviet studies, believes that "pesticides, like radiation, have no bottom threshold of activity: any amount of exposure results, to a greater or lesser extent, in the collapse of the body's immunity system. As a result, the human organism is rendered defenseless in the face of ordinary respiratory and cardiovascular disorders, as well as diseases of the digestive and reproductive organs. When examined closely," continues Yablokov, "all pesticides without exception prove to have either mutagenous or some other kind of negative effect on the natural environment and the human body."[9]

Yablokov stressed the rapid growth of mutations and genetic disorders in many areas throughout the former Soviet Union, especially in Central Asia.

Genetic structures are the final frontier reached by the negative impact of pollution. Homo sapiens is the final link, the final stage in the pyramid of any modern ecosystem. In the case of Central Asia, the situation is deliberately analyzed from the top down; for if deterioration threatens human health, and even survival of the entire human population, then it is simply too late to deal with the flora, the fauna, and the state of the soil.

In Central Asia it is too late to discuss the stability of ecosystems ruled by cotton. Any monoculture leads to the collapse of ecosystems over an area much larger than that where it is actually grown. In the case of cotton, the sphere of influence on adjoining vegetable and fruit plantations is enlarged even further due to the chemicals dispersed through the environment.

Until recently, the true scale of pollution on irrigated fields was glossed over or misrepresented by both the local and the

"Moscow" statistical offices. Glasnost changed the situation somewhat, but an even greater role was played by the very fact that the population continued to grow. In recent years the republics of Central Asia have not been able to supply themselves with even the basic foodstuffs. By 1990 the gap between demand and supply reached 10 percent.[10] With these developments, the burning question could no longer be avoided: how much land is actually cultivated in Central Asia, and by what means, and how much of it is devoted to cotton plantations?

Virtually all researchers concurred in viewing the cotton monoculture as the obvious cause of the Aral disaster, a disaster so obvious that it can be depicted graphically and geographically, with the "arrow of evil" launched from Moscow, by the system of centralized planning, into the heart of Central Asia—the Aral.[11] Many found reasons to hope for an improvement in the situation. Gorbachev, whose policy of glasnost lifted the veil of secrecy from the gruesome figures on infant mortality in areas of intensive cotton production, could not confine the issue to the realm of discussion alone. But the situation in Central Asia has shown no signs of improvement. Rather, the opposite: the problems of monoculture have proved to reach deeper than the roots of the cotton plant.

Doubt No. 1: The scene is the Zirat cemetery on the shore of the former Aral Sea. . . . To the sounds of an ancient dirge, a *zhoktau,* a grave is being dug by a group of Kazakhs from the village of Zirat, who are burying a relative, or rather, trying to bury. The bottom of the grave is filled with water. With resigned persistence, the people shovel out the black slush, but the bottom fills with water once again. This happens in many places throughout the Aral basin; the sea has dried out, but the soil is saturated with brackish, stagnant water. The film director Azimov, who came to the funeral of a relative and was stunned by this scene, went on to make a film about how a lifetime is too short for some to grasp the simplest ecological causes.

Where does all this water in the earth come from? Why is it here, when there is so little of it around?

Although here the ecological chain of causality is even shorter and simpler than in the North, the social and economic causes are much more intricate. True, the cotton fields soak up sixty cubic kilometers of water out of the ninety cubic kilometers used in irrigation, yet only a third of that water actually reaches the plants; the remaining two-thirds are allowed to go to waste, to seep into the ground. The groundwater rises to the surface, forming swamps and salt marshes.

How much water does Central Asian cotton actually require? Soviet experts believed that irrigation in general claimed nearly 90 cubic kilometers of water out of the estimated 120–127 cubic kilometers that comprise the overall river volume in the area. Of these 90 cubic kilometers, approximately 60–65 are used for cotton. The area produces 6.5 million tons of cotton per year, and the amount of water required to produce one kilogram of raw cotton averages approximately ten cubic meters.

If we compare these ten cubic meters per kilogram with the analogous figures for other countries with similar climatic conditions but more advanced technologies, the contrast will be striking. For example, in Israel the average ratio is 1.2–1.3 cubic meters of water to one kilogram of cotton; adding another 0.2 cubic meters of water lost through seepage will bring the figure to around 1.5 cubic meters per kilogram. The difference between the average figures for Israel and Central Asia comes to 660 percent![12] What could explain such a disparity?

The list of reasons is rather long. It is headed by irrigation canals that are dug directly in the earth; for Uzbekistan this means 150,000 kilometers out of the total of 157,000. Next are the primitive means of irrigation, which, together with the inferior canals, bring the efficiency factor to as low as 0.3–0.35 (as compared with Israel's 0.9). The situation is exacerbated further by the policy of cost-free water, with the accompanying wasteful use of water in irrigation. The share of modern technology in Uzbekistan's irrigation is 15–20 percent; for other republics the number is even smaller.

In principle, the 6.5 million tons of cotton produced in Central Asia could be grown by using no more than 25 to 31 cubic kilometers of water instead of the present 60 cubic kilometers. The rapid increase in irrigated areas began in the early 1950s; had it been accompanied by a parallel development of modern water-saving technology, the overall consumption of water used in irrigation could have remained on the level of the 1950s, which would have kept the level of the Aral Sea at the safe mark.[13]

However, more relevant evidence is provided by some experiments that were conducted in Uzbekistan and Tajikistan within the framework of the existing kolkhoz system. These experiments prove that it was possible to reduce the amount of water used in producing cotton by 30 to 60 percent, mainly by charging for the use of water, without having to introduce modern technologies and new varieties of cotton. That is quite a reduction, and one that could be obtained today. A reduction in water consumption could reduce the labor force by 6–12 percent. But do the kolkhozes and sovkhozes throughout Central Asia really want to cut down their labor force? The answer is an emphatic no. The most widely used technique of irrigation "by furrows" may be extremely backward, often causing enormous overexpenditure of water, soil erosion, and salination; yet in the eyes of the local population is has the overriding advantage of requiring a large work force.

The cotton-producing industry in Central Asia uses up too much labor, and the labor efficiency continues to drop. However, modernizing any sector of the cotton industry, including irrigation, would bring about increasing unemployment, already a sharply felt problem in these republics.

The water used to irrigate cotton fields may reach the height of up to five meters during a season. Yet the same amount of water could be used on fruit or vegetable plantations. The reason is the same: more water means more jobs.

Recently there has been a marked effort to step up the construction of plumbing systems in Uzbekistan, Tajikistan, and

Turkmenia, in order to supply at least part of the population with pure drinking water. (This project was financed by Moscow.) An eyewitness gave the following account: "In Tajik villages, all new plumbing comes without water taps. . . . In water fountains and homes, water simply pours out 24 hours a day. There are no taps to be had; they are not manufactured in Tajikistan."[14]

A resource vitally important for the Tajik people is being destroyed, and the simplest thing would be to blame Moscow again, the State Planning Committee, for having failed to meet the demand for taps. We could certainly voice our accusations, but would this really advance our understanding of the problems facing Central Asia?

Doubt No. 2, and Others: Careless squandering of water reserves raises doubt that monoculture alone can explain Central Asia's disastrous predicament; there are additional reasons for skepticism.

Cotton is a crop that requires a maximum of pesticides wherever it is grown. This suggests that reduction of cotton fields in Central Asia will to some extent help reduce pesticide pollution of the human environment. However, pesticides and chemical fertilizers are needed not only for cotton but also for fruit and vegetables, whose production is actively promoted by supporters of environmental protection. In Moldavia, southern Ukraine, and the northern Caucasus—cotton-free areas producing mainly fruit, vegetables, and rice—both environmental pollution and the amount of toxic residues in the produce are still extremely high. According to press reports, in some rice-growing parts of the Krasnodar region the incidence of cancer increases at an annual average of 5.4 to 10 percent, while 55.6 to 60 percent of all babies suffer from inborn pathological disorders. "We, the residents of the Krasnoarmeiskii district," states one letter to *Literaturnaia gazeta,* "feel that we are in the middle of chemical warfare, and the enemy has no intention of stopping it."[15]

On maps illustrating statistics on infant illness in the former Soviet Union, Moldavia and the southern parts of Ukraine and

Russia are almost as red as the cotton-growing republics of Central Asia and Azerbaijan. Analogous results of chemical pollution are observed in many Third World countries with developing modern agriculture, such as India, El Salvador, and Nicaragua. As the analysis points out, here the decisive factor is not so much cotton, nor the cost of pesticides and fertilizers: in India farmers have to pay for every kilo of chemicals, while Soviet collective farms get them practically for nothing. The main problem is the lack of an efficient system of environmental control, in addition to various social factors, above all the poor quality of education. DDT, expressly prohibited by the Ministry of Public Health many years ago, has been steadily used to this day by the veterinary service in Kazakhstan and Turkmenia. Local herdsmen, whom no one has bothered to warn against the danger of DDT, mix it with water and rub the white paste into their faces to keep away mosquitoes.[16]

In effect, the modern use of mineral fertilizers and pesticides in agriculture has proved to be one form of high technology whose application presents a real difficulty in developing countries.

It is worth noting that the average Soviet citizen has an instinctive distrust of the quality of any Soviet-made product. For example, while mixing paint bought in a store, he is more than likely to exceed the proportions recommended by the instructions, so as to ensure effective results. Indeed, what person with any self-respect and an experience of using Soviet-made materials and equipment would actually obey the instruction to "dilute two grams of powdered pesticide in 100 liters of water"? He will double or triple the dose at the very least.

Many new laboratories have been set up for the purpose of determining the level of toxic residues in food. However, the Central Asian newspaper *Pravda Vostoka* ran an article about cases of dangerous poisoning from some watermelons that had allegedly been checked in a laboratory. Large shipments of fruit and vegetables that were cleared through their respective kolkhoz and sovkhoz laboratories were found in independent tests to contain excessive amounts of chemicals. According to the same newspaper, only 1.7 percent of all fruits and vegetables that pass through government laboratories are reported to contain nitrates, while a selective test conducted by experts discovered nitrates in 22 cases out of 40.[17] Early in 1989 Pravda published the results of a study that had found 12 percent of all food, including meat and milk products, in Kazakhstan and 18.97 percent in Tajikistan to contain toxic chemicals; and the percentage continues to grow.[18]

True to established tradition, in using fertilizers and pesticides farmers throughout Central Asia revert to a double standard: "for private use" and "for sale." Vegetables, fruit, and rice delivered to the state or sold on the market receive much greater doses of chemicals than those kept for "private use." The general level of farmers' awareness is demonstrated by the fact that Turkmenia's Deputy Minister of Public Health, D. Tesler, asked journalists to advise the populace, "For the vegetables grown on your own plots for your own children, please do not use nitric fertilizers."[19]

Yet the task of raising the level of education among the farm population in Central Asia is far from simple. "Let's face it," wrote Moscow economist I. Bogdanov in the Tashkent magazine *Zvezda Vostoka*, "the village school in Uzbekistan is incapable of teaching anyone anything." No one tried to argue with Bogdanov, and the reasons for this situation are widely known: the entire system of education is in an extremely backward state, comparable only to the state of the public health system. Meanwhile, some 60 percent of Uzbekistan's population are educated in village schools. Upon graduation they are the ones expected to work with modern irrigation technology where the quantities of water and chemicals are determined by computers. How can a school that barely manages to teach its students to read and write be expected to give them even a basic knowledge of chemistry, biology, or medicine? There is bitter irony in the fact that environmental pollution, whose elements children in village schools find so difficult to grasp, is the very factor that has impeded their understanding. Specialists find a direct link between pollution and the growing rate of anemia and hypertrophy among children and believe that it impairs even further their already flagging progress.

Pesticides have already caused grave damage to the genetic health of Central Asians. Even if we imagine a hypothetical situation in which, starting today, pesticides were excluded from use on cotton or any other fields, the rate of mutations in the following generations would continue to rise due to the increasing probability of combining two latent defective genes. In this respect, the rate of defective newborns is no longer dependent on ecological but totally on social factors. In Central Asian republics the payment of *kalym,* a bride price, is still a widely practiced tradition, even though it exceeds by far the annual income of an average village family. Since marriages among close relatives require no *kalym,* there is an increasing tendency to enter such marriages.

Shirin Turaeva, a genetics expert from Turkmenia, claims that in some areas the incidence of tribal and intrafamily marriages ranges between 10 and 60 percent. In her opinion, reducing the number of such marriages would bring infant mortality down by half within one generation, as well as cause a drastic decrease in mental retardation.[20]

Who Needs All This Cotton? Paradoxically, the more far-reaching Gorbachev's reforms became, the more counterproductive they proved to be for the Central Asian environment.

In 1988 production plans were reduced; yet satellite photos taken in 1989 showed that cotton in Central Asia took up more land than required by the plan—23,000 hectares above the rigid quotas imposed by Moscow! How could this be accounted for? Who stands to benefit from the dictatorship of cotton? For, despite everything, someone must profit from cotton.

It is not hard to guess who that someone is. One of the first "discoveries" of glasnost was the Uzbekistan mafia; in 1985–86, thousands of its members were arrested, including dozens of top-ranking party officials. It was conclusively proven that the billions wielded by the mafia had been gained primarily from the cotton industry.

Indeed, a more lucrative source of illegal profit would be difficult to imagine. Cotton is a relatively costly product, manufactured everywhere and in huge quantities. The customer placing the order, the supplier of technology and equipment, and the buyer were all one and the same—the government, with almost unlimited financial means at its disposal.

The first link in the chain is the job of inspector at a cotton-treatment factory. Until Gorbachev's "purges" it had cost up to a million rubles to secure this job. After five years of perestroika the price had risen to two million. The oriental saying "He who handles the honey gets to lick his fingers" is a rather accurate explanation why the "honeycomb" retained its size.

In the end, the Moscow authorities were powerless to prevent the widespread corruption in Central Asia's militia and armed forces, which supplied weapons to the mafia and the nationalist factions. But the question is not whether today's mafia wields unlimited powers; obviously, it is powerful enough to torpedo state instructions, whether they concern a reduction in cotton-growing areas or anything else. Why should the mafia, together with its party allies, give up its profits? The only reason to relinquish the cotton industry, with its assured system of making money, would be in exchange for a yet more lucrative business. This business is the drug trade.

Narcotic plants, such as hemp and poppies, flourish even on washed-out, meager soil and require little water. There are clear indications that drug production and drug trafficking, tightly linked to the South Asian drug trade, are playing an increasingly important role in the mafia's operations. Still, drugs have not yet replaced cotton as a source of profit; the two coexist. The main market for opium and heroin had been considered to be the large cities in the European part of the USSR; more recently, however, it has been reported that of all the republics, Turkmenia has the largest percentage of drug addicts.

The mafia in Central Asia represents what may be the first major case of such a group actually contributing to environmental destruction and destabilization of a sizable part of the globe. Until now, the history of environmental pollution has witnessed analogous examples on a much more modest scale. The Corsican mafia, for example, sabotaged a ban on hunting a rare species of bird, since the ban involved a prohibition on carrying firearms. Another example, on a larger scale this time, is the use of thousands of tons of sulphuric acid and other chemicals by the drug cartels in Colombia. These chemicals, used in underground laboratories for the primary treatment of coca leaves, are later dumped— naturally, without being neutralized in any way—into rivers and ditches.

A more thorough study leads to the realization that the squandering of water and mineral resources has, as its underlying cause, not so much the dictatorship of cotton as unemployment and steep population growth. The dumping of lethal doses of poison into the water and soil can be traced ultimately to the impoverished and backward educational system, and the incidence of retarded babies to the traditions of Muslim society. Moreover, there is a force that is quite successful in preserving, protecting, and encouraging these trends, for what is suicidal from the point of view of national interests has been quite profitable for the party mafia.

Where Does the Social End and the Ecological Begin? The Aral disaster is a combined result of a series of ecological blunders (wasteful irrigation, pesticide pollution of water and soil) and social factors (unchecked population growth, unemployment, inferior education, the conservatism and clannishness of the local society). That is why a map of ecological disasters unfolding in Central Asia should be based not on cotton production or even regional economic data but rather on social instability in the region.

Sergei Poliakov, an ethnographer who has studied Central Asia for over twenty-five years, believes that the social situation in Central Asia is fundamentally unstable for historical reasons. "When we created the national states which have been and still are such a source of pride in these republics, we laid the delayed-action mine that has been triggered today. By adopting ethnic origins as the cornerstone, we isolated the links of a unified economic mechanism." Had this mechanism been used as the foundation of the state structure, some consideration would have been given to the unique ecological features of the areas located in the Aral basin. Poliakov continues:

> We introduced medicine but failed to come up with a reasonable policy of birth control. Now, to satisfy Central Asia's need for potable water we would somehow have to obtain a cubic kilometer of water a year. In the village of Varukh in the Andijan Region the population grows at an annual rate of 9 percent. In such a situation, people cannot be assured of normal living conditions without a highly developed industry. But there is no industry in the Andijan region that could create 300 new jobs, ten day-care centers, or ten school classes per day. I am exaggerating a little. But the region's population grows by 300 people daily. Twenty-five percent of women in the Fergana valley actually give birth twice a year. The rate of infant mortality in Central Asia is as high as 50, and in some areas up to 300 deaths for every thousand newborns. Today 30 percent of babies are born with genetic defects; that is an official figure. This is the result not only of ecological but also of genetic degeneration (intrafamilial marriages are common since the *kalym* is smaller). The data I am using are not available in official reports; they were obtained by means of a technique we developed and have been tested against events—whether "interethnic" clashes or ecological disasters—which we predicted on this basis.

According to Poliakov, the clashes that first broke out in 1989 among Kyrgyz, Uzbeks, Tajiks, and other groups over water, plots of land, and other issues are proof that the hatred and mutual resentment pent up over the years will not be conducive to improvement in the situation. And, he adds, "We are facing a catastrophe not only in Central Asia but in Russia as well. Given the demographic and ecological situation, a part of Central Asia will flood into Russia, there to create ethnic, social, and other kinds of conflicts."[21]

Poliakov is not alone in his prognosis. Other demographers and sociologists have warned that even today's extensive agriculture will not be able to provide jobs and food to an annual increase of 450–600 thousand people seeking employment and livelihood. There is a need for rapid urbanization, but the cities are already filled to overcrowding with former villagers who are neither professionally nor psychologically prepared to tackle city life. These cities are a powder keg of suppressed violence and extremism ready to explode.[22]

Given the increasing problems of the urban centers—lack of living space, inferior sanitary services, a shortage of drinking water, and, above all, a growth in drug trafficking and organized crime—the next stage must be a "brain drain" from cities becoming unfit for normal life. This will be accompanied by a mass surge of refugees into "richer" areas, and into European countries whenever possible. Whether we label this a flood of ecological refugees or an exodus of some other kind is of little importance. We are still faced with a collapse of social structures, a situation that imperils not only the Central Asian republics but Russia as well.

"So what happens now?" wonders one Soviet researcher, having demonstrated the sluggish inertia of a managerial system that "sucks dry" all the resources, down to the last drop of fresh water. Then he answers his own question: "What happens now is exactly what is happening in the Aral basin."[23]—in other words, depletion of water sources, desertification of lands, which will become unfit for cultivation, where people will be unwilling, and then unable, to live.

It has been mentioned that primitive methods of irrigation of cotton fields play a crucial role in salination, soil erosion, and further desertification. However, "in northern Kara-Kum," writes A. Monin, a corresponding member of the USSR Academy of Sciences, "the accepted practice is to abandon fields as they become salinated, and move on to adjacent plots. If you drive along the Khiva–Tashauz–Nukus route, you will see snow-white steppes,

Table 3

Projected Population of the Former Soviet Republics for the Year 2029
(in millions of people)

	1989	2029
Russia	146.8	152.1
Ukraine	52.1	51.5
Belarus	10.2	10.9
Uzbekistan	20.6	51.6
Moldova	4.4	5.9
Georgia	5.5	6.7
Armenia	3.6	5.3
Azerbaijan	7.4	12.6
Estonia	1.5	1.6
Lithuania	3.6	4.0
Latvia	2.6	2.6
Kazakhstan	17.6	32.5
Kirghizia	4.5	9.9
Tajikistan	5.4	13.5
Turkmenia	3.7	9.7

Source: A. Avdeev and I. Troitskii, "Demograficheskii aspekty razvitiia ekonomiki na rubezhe XXI veka," *Planovoe khoziaistvo*, 1990, no. 12, p. 55.

a lifeless plain stretching in both directions as far as the eye can see. We must face the truth: it appears that these salt marshes are here for good."[24]

Monin was describing rice paddies rather than cottonfields. Still, salination of any kind may be the most irreparable type of desertification. But by far the most devastating in scope is the pasture type—uncontrolled grazing of cattle that lays bare enormous parcels of land. This is a common practice throughout Central Asia, Kazakhstan, and even adjoining regions; yet the situation is the gravest in central Turkmenia and the Kazakh steppes all the way to Kalmykia on the northern Caspian coast.

Tractors, trucks, and other vehicles running, without any order or supervision, all over the semidesert areas with highly sensitive vegetation are the main cause of yet another type of desertification—the technogenous. Destroyed vegetation is quickly replaced by sand. Due to the shortage of cooking fuel, forests in the rural areas of Turkmenia and Tajikistan are destroyed at a speed that exceeds by far the rate of deforestation projects conducted by the state.

Sociologists may study various aspects of population increase, educational problems, or the influence of tradition and life-style on industrial relations. Ecologists may concentrate on various kinds of pollution (water, air, soil, the sea). Ministries may exercise their control over each separate aspect (which is what they actually do most of the time). But there is a process that ignores the nuances of the internal chain of cause and effect, compounds the effects of social and ecological collapse, and reminds us that practice is the ultimate yardstick. In practice, desertification is the end result of mass pollution and contamination of the environment. Desertification constitutes the combined effect of all visible and invisible disruptions of natural resources.

In the mechanism of desertification taking place in Uzbekistan, Turkmenia, Kazakhstan, and neighboring areas, we can find the same four basic stages as in the processes under way in the North.

The encroachment of desertified areas on the still normal and productive ones manifests itself primarily in changes in the level of subterranean waters. When the expansion comes from a real sand desert, the level sharply drops; when, however, the encroaching land is what used to be (or still is) an irrigated cotton or rice field, the level of subterranean waters rapidly rises. Given the primitive irrigation methods, subterranean salt water, which in many places runs only five or six meters deep, rises to the surface. As this water evaporates, its salt level increases, the salt crystallizes, and the soil is turned into salt marsh.

Another specific feature of the "southern" type of desertification is the massive influence of pesticides and other water-diluted chemicals on the soil flora and fauna. Deprived of these crucial components, the soil loses its fertility and then its structure (although, when there is no salination, fertility is not lost for good; under favorable conditions this soil can be restored). In all other aspects, just as in tundra ecosystems, the impact of an extensive collapsed territory lowers the stability of its "victim."

When an ecosystem is affected to a significant degree, a few additional destabilizing endogenous or exogenous factors—such as cattle overgrazing or a drought—are enough to cause the productive ecosystem to collapse. The impact on the neighboring, still "normal" system increases, and the process of degradation goes on. It may pass unnoticed temporarily, but when another year of drought or an ill-conceived irrigation or industrial development project provides another "push," another ecosystem collapses.

According to A. Reteium, a Soviet geographer, biological productivity of ecosystems throughout most of Central Asia has gone down by 30–50 percent; many rivers and lakes have disappeared altogether; and the total area of sand deserts has grown by over 100,000 square kilometers. "We are looking at every sign of a crisis," he writes, "with the situation becoming uncontrollable."[25]

The Kara-Kum and the Kyzyl-Kum, the ancient "nucleus" of Central Asian deserts and semideserts, occupy roughly 700,000 square kilometers, or less than 22 percent of the total area of Uzbekistan, Turkmenia, and Kazakhstan. By now, active desertification has claimed an additional 35–40 percent of the area, and the expanding tendency manifests itself in the center (around the "nucleus") as well as in the periphery. Each year the desert swallows from 800,000 to 1,100,000 hectares in the very heartland of the Asian continent.[26]

There is only one area in the world where the destructive desertification processes advance on an even larger scale than in Central Asia and its vicinity, and that is the Sahara and the Sahel. There, roughly 1.5 million hectares of land turn into desert each year. Yet when we recall that the overall area of the Sahel is much greater than that of Central Asia and Kazakhstan, we see that the rate of desertification in Central Asia is proportionately even larger than in Africa.

Until now no one has spoken about a Sahara being formed in Central Asia; but one Soviet ecologist insists that the expansion of deteriorated areas that have lost almost all biological productivity can be called, with every good reason, "sahelization."[27]

Admittedly, "sahelization," or rapid expansion of totally deteriorated ecosystems, can advance only given the existence of a "Sahara" that is the moving force behind the whole process. In fact,
such a Sahara, threatening both land and water—lakes and even
seas, like the Caspian—already exists at the heart of Eurasia.

4

The Dust of the Invasion

Forty years ago, experts began to realize that the North was actually moving south. The northern cold, and above all the northern wasteland, was pushing toward the forests and sparse forests, while the tundra and forest tundra were advancing south, moving closer and closer to Central Asia and China. The crucial role of the huge belt of taiga and forests as a stabilizing factor in all ecological processes has already been discussed. It is also worth mentioning that, after the tropical forests of the Amazon, the Siberian taiga is the largest source of oxygen on the planet.

About twenty years ago, the South, too, began seriously to encroach on the North. Central Asian deserts, as they expanded, caused the steppes of southern Kazakhstan to dry up; the summer in this area became noticeably hotter. On the other hand, it would not be true to say that signs of desertification appeared in the westerly direction only. The desert made itself felt also at the opposite end of Central Asia—the east with the thinning and disappearing forests at the foothills of Kopet-Dag and Tyan-Shan, and the receding vegetation cover on hillsides that had been ploughed up without any prior tests by specialists, and contrary to the time-proven experience of the local residents.

The dismal results of ecological collapse, which, as we have seen in the case of Central Asia, are multiplied by social collapse, make us view with skepticism the projects intended to restore the Aral Sea to its former value as a freshwater reservoir.

In order to return the Aral to the boundaries it occupied in the past, and, more importantly, to help the area regain the vitality it had a few decades ago, a minimum of 40–50 cubic kilometers of water would be required annually. Yet this is impossible—primarily for social reasons. Just as in the past, social and not ecological causes keep the necessary water from reaching the Aral.

In the fall of 1988 the Soviet government passed a resolution which gave the go-ahead for the construction of hundreds of kilometers of new canals. This time their purpose was not to irrigate but to rechannel into the Aral all the surplus water left after irrigation. Previously this water, containing large amounts of salt, mineral fertilizers, and pesticides, was dumped into land depressions, forming dozens of stagnant salt lakes. Some of these lakes—Sarykamysh, Sichankul, Dengikul—now extend up to hundreds of square kilometers.

The available official and unofficial reports give no clear indication as to the results of this project or the amount of water the new canals may have added to the Aral, so it would be difficult to provide an accurate picture of the project's present state. But from the very start, the authors of the canal project ran into a problem never before encountered by anyone in the world. Here, the unique nature of the Aral disaster appeared in its full magnitude: the problem was not so much the shortage of water as its pollution.

"The water of Sarykamysh and other lakes contains tens of millions of tons of salts and poisonous chemicals," warned Dr. Shalkat Umarov. "If this water flows out, you can imagine what it will carry into the Aral; still, most of the 'chemical' layer will remain on the bottom. . . . As the lakes dry up, the thousands of square kilometers of exposed bottom will turn into new sources of poisonous dust storms. . . . We must continue to water these monsters," concludes Umarov, "to keep them from killing us off."[1]

"To keep them from killing us off. . . ." I believe that the literal meaning of this phrase is even deeper and gloomier than the

image it evokes. In essence, it encourages Central Asia to continue along its destructive path, to waste more water through primitive irrigation, in order to "water the monster"—all this with the full knowledge that the day will come when there is no more water to pour, and a monster far more terrible will burst out in many places at once. It is too late to save the Aral, so now we must save ourselves from it—that seems to be the implication.

Is there a way to save ourselves from the Aral? Paradoxically enough, there is, and it is not by running away. The paradox of the solution lies in its simplicity and low cost, coupled with the fact that it does not threaten the interests of the party mafia or the population. The idea is to cover the dry Aral bottom with plants resistant to the salts produced by saline soil. Professor Kurochkina, a member of the Kazakh Academy of Sciences, has demonstrated through tests that the plants she had selected would take root and provide a reliable ground cover, provided the soil contained water, even if it is salinated and polluted.[2] In other words, a timely effort aimed at preventing the sea's entire bottom from turning into a sand desert would make it possible to create a vegetation cover, which would halt (or significantly reduce) emission of salts and poisonous chemicals, as well as soften the climatic effect of newly created deserts that used to be the seabed. Of course, the plant cover grown through Kurochkina's technique would bear no resemblance to the forests or even the thick shrubbery, the *tugai*, that grew only a short time ago in the delta of the Amu-Darya and the Syr-Darya. Still, this scant-looking vegetation could achieve results similar to the no less "scant" lichens in the tundra—namely, stabilize the ecosystems about to collapse. It could put a brake on the desertification that is transforming the heart of Asia into a Sahara.

It could—but will it actually happen? This question raises the same doubts that exist in connection with reforestation efforts in India, Africa, and other Third World countries. The hundreds of grassroots Green groups that recently emerged in those areas have been planting trees, encouraging ecological education in local communities, and introducing numerous other projects.

Still, as Alan Durning pointed out in his 1989 analysis of the situation, "small can be beautiful, but it can also be insignificant."[3]

Even when compared to Third World countries, the Green movement in Central Asia is on a very modest scale. None of the republics has managed to establish an ecological network. This is not to ignore the fact that rudiments of a Green movement are appearing in Central Asia, and that every political movement and party, including Muslim fundamentalists, refers to ecological issues (though mainly as evidence of abuses of Central Asia). The growing availability of ecological information, the publications evoking the traditionally respectful attitude of the *dekhkan* (peasant) toward water and land, the tree-planting ceremonies during the Navruz folk festival, the street-cleaning campaigns—all these are decades, even generations away from a system of environmental protection capable of neutralizing, not to say reversing, the destructive inertia of developing agriculture and industry. Until now, inertia has had the better chance of success.

Thus, to judge by the available data, the dubious and costly project of laying canals to rechannel surplus irrigation water has been put into effect with much more zeal than the immeasurably cheaper planting projects proposed by Kurochkina. Dr. Kurochkina herself is pessimistic in her view of the situation, at least for the immediate future. She believes that too little is being done; meanwhile, desertification is now destroying Lake Balkhash, and the Caspian Sea faces the threat of disastrous pollution.[4]

The danger, according to Kurochkina, is moving toward the Caspian from the northeast, where the oil and gas industry is rapidly developing, and a dam is being built to separate the vast shallow-water areas from the main sea.

During the miners' strike in the spring of 1991, those newspapers still loyal to Gorbachev gave a good deal of attention to rapid development of the new and rich Tengiz oil field, located on the northeast shore of the Caspian. Reportedly, an annual output of 35–45 million tons of oil would provide a much needed boost to the Soviet power industry, deteriorating because of the strikes, "Green" opposition to the construction of new atomic power stations, and a host of other reasons.

The fact that the figure of 35–45 million tons was probably exaggerated for propaganda purposes is not that important in the ecological context. The relevant point is that the production and treatment of even the 12 million tons of oil per year quoted in earlier, official reports on the Soviet-American agreement was formidable enough, considering the ecological impact of the oil and gas industry.

It is estimated that the Tengiz field contains 25 billion barrels, making it one of the world's largest oil deposits. During Gorbachev's visit to the United States in the spring of 1990, a $10 billion agreement on development of the Tengiz oil and gas projects was signed. The company involved was Chevron.

Chevron's involvement in the development of the Tengiz field had begun in November 1988. In that same year, the Soviet Petroleum Ministry had signed a protocol of intent with four Western corporations (Occidental, Enichem, Montedison, and Marubeni) for a joint venture to develop and operate a petrochemical complex using gas from Tengiz. The complex was to produce various plastics and commercial-grade sulfur. Prior to the agreement with Chevron, the petrochemical project was reported to be the largest Soviet joint venture with Western firms.[5]

The northeastern part of the Caspian, where the oil and gas deposit was discovered ten years ago, lies next to the "nucleus of Central Asian deserts," which has been steadily expanding thanks to the eco-domino effect. The area of the oil deposits is a semidesert abounding in salt lakes. Track vehicles provide the main means of transportation in the open areas of Central Asia, just as in the tundra. As construction proceeds in the oil fields, land rovers and tractors are destroying the scant and weak vegetation cover, facilitating the rapid advance of erosion. Dust storms, the area's permanent scourge, carry thousands of tons of dust into the Caspian Sea from the oil fields.[6]

The harsh continental climate (with seasonal temperatures ranging from −40° C in the winter to +40° C in the summer) speeds up the process of desertification. This factor alone ought to be sufficient to set off the "red light." However, this component, crucial in its own right, is relegated to a secondary role in the interplay of yet more powerful factors—the unique features of the deposit itself and the unstable boundary between sea and land throughout the area north of the Caspian.

What are the deposit's unique features? The oil lies at a depth of 5,000–5,500 meters; its pressure reaches 910 atmospheres, with temperatures of 107°C to 125°C. Up to 25 percent of the oil's total volume is made up of gas (hydrogen sulfide). In 1986, what was probably the biggest gusher in the history of oil exploration burst out of one of the test wells. This sparked a fire which was also one of the worst of its kind in world history before the Kuwait fires. The fire, which raged for nearly fourteen months, was eventually put out with the help of American experts.

This incident convinced the Soviet government that without foreign assistance Tengiz oil could bring more harm than good. Contracts were signed first with Hungarian specialists, and later with Chevron, which had the experience of working with similar dangerous deposits in San Ramon, California. Company representatives also promised to supply the best available facilities to prevent air and water pollution.[7]

Chevron may have experience, but there is a problem that remains unsolved. Even at a considerable distance from shore, the Caspian Sea is quite shallow—no deeper than 1–1.5 meters. In recent years there has been a noticeable rise in the water table, accompanied by the sinking of the land at the rate of 3–5 millimeters per year. As a result, if in 1986 one of the Tengiz deposits lay 16 kilometers offshore, in 1989 the distance was reduced to a mere 5 kilometers! A few times a year, strong winds cause the sea to swell, driving it a few kilometers inland. The solution proposed is to build, at the cost of one billion rubles, a dam separating the shallow water from the open sea, to serve as a barrier against the advance of pollution.

The project of building such a dam in the Caspian has a dangerous precedent. Only a few years ago, a dam was built across the huge Bay of Kara-Bogaz-Gol. Its purpose was to cut down the losses due to water evaporation, and to help stop the falling sea level. In three years the bay dried up; the former sea bottom, just like in the Aral, turned into a sand desert.[8]

At the works managed by Chevron in California, rates of pollution do not exceed the rather stringent local standards. So it seems that Chevron can achieve significant reductions in air and water pollution. But would Chevron's purifying technology prove to be efficient within a Soviet social environment, a Soviet system of using technology and resources?

A mere 300 kilometers northeast of Tengiz, from the opposite edge, the Astrakhan gas-condensing plant is using the resources of the same oil and gas deposit. Among other Western equipment, the plant has bought a French-made computerized system of production control, which was intended to reduce emissions of gas into the atmosphere. However, in many production units the basic temperature and pressure gauges are missing and the automatic blocking systems have been disconnected. As a result, the computerized system is virtually manually operated, and gas concentrations in the adjoining settlements are so high that some residents regularly use gas masks.[9]

Neither the health services nor other local authorities signed any documents allowing the Astrakhan plant to be put into operation. Nevertheless, the plant is functioning (and there are plans to double its output), as the management claims, by force of the ecological imperative: only gas produced by the plant can replace the heavy oil used in heating, and thus relieve the acute problem of air pollution in many large cities.

Already, the air and water pollution in the Tengiz area presents such a grave problem that at the beginning of 1989 the USSR Environmental Protection Committee managed to secure a freeze on the financing of the Tengiz project. Besides citing the high disease rate among the population, committee experts pointed out that the consequences of an accident, whether due to an earthquake or some other cause, at an oil field with a planned annual yield of 12 million tons of oil would be potentially similar to the consequences of the Chernobyl disaster. The quantities of hydrogen sulfide that could burst out of an oil well would endanger human lives and everything living within dozens or even hundreds of kilometers. Such emissions of gas, likely to be accompanied by fires, would affect the quality of the atmosphere throughout the northern hemisphere.[10]

Just as in Astrakhan, the authorities agreed with the ecologists, but the Tengiz project went full speed ahead. Now, the independent Kazakhstan pushes it. And once again, the ecological imperative is cited: without oil and gas, the environmental situation in many parts of the CIS would only grow worse. This claim may have some merit; at least, it cannot be dismissed outright as pure fabrication. But it does not take an especially acute observer to detect a common denominator, a shared tendency, in every area of the CIS where ecological imperatives have the upper hand. On Yamal and in Astrakhan, in Tengiz and in Central Asia, oil, gas, and water are being wasted, and the environment is being destroyed, because without these resources the ecological situation will be even worse tomorrow. Large cities will be totally asphyxiated by coal smoke; or a terrible jinn will rise up from the bottom of poisonous lakes. Even so, the fact is that the situation *is* getting worse; if areas like Yamal and Tengiz are threatened with extinction today, then "tomorrow" is hardly a relevant issue.

The ecological instability of Yamal and Tengiz—two major sources of energy so badly needed by the collapsing Soviet economy—may be viewed as a fatal piece of bad luck. One could also look for—and find—profoundly rational explanations, such as the depletion of almost all the cheap and easily accessible natural resources; or claim that Yamal and Tengiz have not been developed until now precisely because of their complexity and vulnerability. Yet in this case it might be more logical to refer to the old and simple adage: Troubles never come alone. In our ecological context, it could be rephrased: Troubles cannot come otherwise than in a long chain.

It would be difficult to invent a more dangerous pattern for a disaster area than the one existing in the Aral and Caspian sea regions. Step by step, the ecosystems in the Tengiz area are collapsing and merging with deserts around the Aral Sea; by now, the distance between Tengiz and the mass of "real" sand deserts has shrunk to a mere 100–150 kilometers. Next to Tengiz lie polluted shallow waters; 400 kilometers to the south is the disaster area of Kara-Bogaz-Gol; 400 kilometers to the northwest there is Kalmykia, arching around the Caspian—Kalmykia, which once was synonymous with "magnificent steppes" but now can only be described by the word "desert."

Reckless year-round cattle pasturing, which used to be done on a seasonal basis, in winter, has led to the formation of the first sand desert in European territory. Its present size is estimated at 7,000 square kilometers, and it is growing by about 10 percent per year. The area, which contains several million hectares of formerly fertile pastures, is rapidly deteriorating. This is not surprising, since, according to Lansat data, up to twenty sheep graze in an area big enough to support only one. Experts have warned that the Kalmyk steppes "are systematically being transformed by man into a sand desert." Yet the misuse goes on.[11]

Raging sandstorms are becoming an increasingly common occurrence in the northern part of the Caspian. In winter the dust is carried as far as Moscow, where snow is covered with a layer of yellow coating, a tell-tale sign of its Asian source.

To the south, Kalmykia is joined by the foothills of the Caucasus, an area long famous for its fertile land. By now, 600,000 hectares of this land have been salinated and abandoned for good, a result of irrigation. Since all of the northern Caucasus has been turned into a zone of intensive agriculture, this means extensive use of the entire variety of modern toxic chemicals and fertilizers. In Azerbaijan, for example, the average amount of pesticides used on a hectare of land exceeds by twenty times the figure for the entire country, and 80 percent of these chemicals are of the types defined as highly dangerous—including DDT and similar substances. As early as 1982, researchers discovered the drastic effect of this kind of pollution on the illness rate and genetic health of the local population.

Through subterranean waters and rivers like the Sulak, the Terek, and the Kura, toxic chemicals contaminate a wide stretch of coastal waters of the Caspian Sea. Around Baku and Sumgait, this type of pollution is aggravated by large quantities of oil and chemical wastes from oil-treatment facilities. On the Soviet side of the Caspian coast, the only area left relatively clean and unspoiled is a 250-kilometer stretch in southern Turkmenia. The 500 kilometers of the Iranian coast contain few industrial sites, and the rivers carry relatively small amounts of chemical wastes and urban sewage. Despite the rapidly growing population, the Iranian part of the Caspian still enjoys its main ecological advantage of being far removed from the Volga, the largest source of pollution in the entire basin.

"I don't like to think about this, but the Caspian may soon become a second Aral," says the chairman of Azerbaijan's Environmental Protection Committee. "The main danger is not the drying up—though it exists—but total contamination and desertification of the sea." According to Academician B. Laskorin, an Aral-type disaster could strike the entire basin of the Caspian and the Volga, populated by no less than 100 million people.[12]

The Volga

• "The Volga is being polluted by wastes from the oil and chemical industry as well as agricultural fertilizers at an enormous rate. . . . Many species, primarily the fish, are dying out; plants are becoming extinct; formerly fertile lands are turned into arid deserts; thousands upon thousands of residents lose their health."[13]—S. Konovalov, head of the Institute of Ecology of the Volga Basin.

• "The ecological situation throughout the Volga is so tense that a small additional impact will be enough for the ecosystem to collapse. In the summer of 1988, the air temperature was a few degrees above average—and millions of fish went belly-up, including tens of thousands of sturgeon."[14]—A. Yablokov, the Russian state counselor for ecology and health.

• "The reason for the mass disease and death among the sturgeon population is the immense scale of water pollution, which occasionally exceeds the permissible norm by up to 700 times for oil and 110 times for surface active substances."[15]—V. Lukianenko, professor at the Institute of Fresh Water Biology, Russian Academy of Sciences.

Of course, the largest rate of pollution is registered in the lowest reaches of the Volga, and in its delta just before it joins the Caspian. But the experts say the critical situation is spreading up the basin, creeping toward central Russia like gangrene from a limb to the brain.

The Azov Sea

• "As a weakened man easily succumbs to disease, so damaged ecosystems readily fall victim to various attacking forces. Forty years ago the Azov Sea was the most fertile source of fish on the planet. As a result of dwindling river flow and of industrial and agricultural pollution, by 1988 the sea became totally barren of fish. In 1986 and 1987 the sea was invaded by jellyfish. In the fall of 1988, the mnemiopsis, an inhabitant of the coast of North America, made an appearance, devouring every living creature whose length was under one centimeter. Each cubic meter of water contains up to 1.5 kilograms of mnemiopsis. Without doubt, the Azov Sea will be empty of fish for many years to come."[16]—A. Yablokov.

The Black Sea

• "A word of advice to fishermen: if, around Sevastopol, Novorossiisk, or Batumi, you chance to catch a fish or two, there is no guarantee that it will be edible."—Iu. Michurin, report from the Black Sea Conference, 1990.

Actually, it is quite possible that the sea will soon run out of fish altogether. Its total biomass of mnemiopsis is approaching one billion tons, which is much more than the entire fish mass.

• "If the anthropogenous influence continues on the same scale, by the year 2,000 it will become impossible not only to swim in the sea but to live in its vicinity."—All-Union Sociology and Ecology Conference, held in 1990 in Kerch.

• "If we do not save the sea, the coast will perish. . . ." —Professor V. Neikiv, secretary of the Eco-Forum for Peace, 1990.

• "The Black Sea, on whose fate hang the present and the future of the peoples of Europe and the Black Sea coast. . . . is on the verge of ecological catastrophe."[17]—Black Sea Conference, 1990.

What can we learn from the above remarks about the situation facing the Volga River and the Caspian, Azov, and Black seas? We began by drawing an analogy with the Aral disaster, which was not accidental. The point of the comparison is simple and has already been mentioned: If a sea or a lake deteriorates, it means that the entire basin is in danger, together with the tributaries large and small that flow into the given body of water, the cities and towns along these tributaries, the industry, the fields and farms. Meanwhile, the basins of the Caspian Sea and the Volga, as well as of the rivers flowing into the Azov and Black seas, comprise a considerable, if not the predominant, share of the European part of what was the USSR. What happens now, when the south of this troubled area has given birth to a source of desertification?

By themselves, the 70,000 square kilometers of Kalmyk sand—the first sand desert on the European continent—cannot pose a threat to the stability of either half of Europe or even southern Russia. Despite Kalmykia's catastrophic situation, and the desert's annual growth rate of 10 percent, it is not a threat in itself, but it could trigger a very dangerous process. In order to see this, one need only glance at an ordinary geographical map. If it takes in not only Kalmykia but also the areas lying to the east and the northeast, which have been discussed in this and the preceding chapters, it will become clear that there is a single process uniting all the areas of Central Asia, Kazakhstan, and the southern part of European Russia. Desertification, which originates in the ancient nucleus of the deserts of Kyzyl-Kum and Kara-Kum, as well as around the former Aral Sea, has become the center of the eco-domino process, covering the entire area between lower Volga and the Chinese border.

In the north, Central Asia is enclosed by the belt of Kazakh steppes, while in the south it is edged in by mountain ranges, some of them very high. The Kazakh steppes, themselves suffering from heavy erosion since the time of Khrushchev's Virgin Lands program, can hardly serve as a barrier against the spread of desertification. The situation is different in the south, where the high mountains can provide some kind of protection against the onslaught of the desert. Still, these mountain ranges should not be viewed as a Great Wall of China, since some of the peaks, like the Kopet-Dag on the Iranian border, are not all that formidable. Just behind the Tyan Shan mountains on the Chinese border lie the vast desert expanse of the Talka-Makan and, further north, the Gobi Desert.[18]

If the current process of environmental pollution and desertification is not stopped or at least slowed down, and if the situation does get out of control, then the expansion and merging of old and new deserts over the next decade may actually lead to the formation of an Asian Sahara. The belt of deserts and semi-deserts starting at the eastern outskirts of Europe—the lower Volga and the northern foothills of the Caucasus—will envelop virtually all of Kazakhstan and Central Asia, possibly spreading as far as central China.

If we realize that the "modest" 70,000 square kilometers of Kalmyk sand are backed by an Asian Sahara being formed in Central Asia, just as the small "patches" of newly formed desert in Central Africa are backed by the African Sahara, then Russia's situation will appear much more dangerous. Then the Kalmyk dust on Moscow snow, with its yellowish Asian tint, will appear not as ordinary dirt but as a harbinger of the impending invasion, as inescapable and ruthless as the Mongol horsemen.

5

Ecology Plus . . .

Fifteen years ago, when I began writing my "underground" book, *The Destruction of Nature in the Soviet Union,* I took into my confidence only three trustworthy friends, as well as my wife, who also specialized in ecological problems. The bulk of the data I used came from scientists who were unaware of what I was doing.

One high-ranking specialist was completely frank with me during our meeting, confident that I would not be able to use more than a minuscule part of the information in my work or in the lectures on the environment that I was preparing for educational television. Another, holding a slightly lesser rank, let me borrow two confidential reports that were full of data on the state of the environment in the USSR, also sure that the censors would delete any facts or figures gleaned from the reports that I might be daring enough to repeat. In those times, as one author put it recently, "publishing such a report could have easily landed the author in jail."[1]

In August 1989, at a conference in Goteborg, biologist Aleksei Yablokov cited data that made my book seem "rosy" in comparison.[2] The ecological disaster spreading through the former USSR and with repercussions reaching far beyond Soviet borders had ceased to be a secret. Problems of environmental protection were ranked by Gorbachev (and by Shevardnadze as well) second after global disarmament issues.

I realize that now, after all the documentaries and books and the many articles that have appeared in the Soviet press as well as publications like *The Economist, Time,* and *Newsweek,* it might be reasonable to ask whether there is any need for another "exposé" on the shocking environmental situation in the former Soviet Union. Haven't they now admitted it themselves? Aren't reforms going to transform the socialist economy into a free-market system, permitting the government to create a truly effective environmental protection mechanism?

Of course, officials began to be concerned about the environment for political reasons, if you can call "politics" the state of shock in which Gorbachev and his successors have been functioning since the collapse of communist ideology and the economy, and in the wake of Chernobyl. Nevertheless, they have introduced a whole range of laws and organizational measures and declared their readiness to do everything to prevent an environmental catastrophe. Gorbachev's new thinking has borne fine fruit in the area of international disarmament; might we expect similar results in the sphere of ecological cooperation? In the West the words *disarmament* and *environment* are often uttered in the same breath.

Yet the political and economic crisis that has plagued the USSR and its successors is so acute that it would seem almost preposterous to waste time on environmental issues. Obviously, this is not the time to think about nature; in war one does not stop to mourn bomb-ravaged landscapes and animals mauled by shells. Give the reformers some time; give them a chance. . . .

But times change. The war in the Persian Gulf was the first in which ecological damage was reckoned to be as great, if not greater, than the human casualties. By the same token, the ecological crisis in the former Soviet Union is not just a minor detail of the general crisis, nor even one of the crucial factors, but rather *the major factor in a crisis that should concern the Soviet Union's neighbors.* My opinion is based, first, on the fact that perestroika not only failed to give rise to an "eco-perestroika" but, on the contrary, was accompanied by a marked increase in the pace of environmental destruction, steeper now than it was before Gorbachev; and second, on the dynamics of the eco-domino process, both in its regional and global effects, which until now have been largely ignored.

Eco-Perestroika. Not many years ago, virtually all Western studies of Soviet environmental problems drew the same conclusions, which might be summarized as follows: when the ideological approach to nature is abandoned, and the miserly funds allocated for environmental protection are increased, and laws curbing centralized power have been passed, and a Ministry of Environmental Protection modeled on the American EPA has been created, and freedom of the press and public control over the functioning of state-owned enterprises has been achieved—only then will the ecological situation in the USSR begin to improve.

And indeed, the day finally came when Soviet leaders abandoned the communist ideology; removed the restrictions on access to ecological information; acknowledged the urgent necessity of environmental protection; increased the budgets for combating water, air, and soil pollution; founded an Environmental Protection Committee (headed by Professor Nikolai Vorontsov, not a party member); and a new Supreme Soviet began actively to consider, and to pass, environmental legislation. And not only this: "Green" groups, organizations, and parties emerged all over the country.

Well then, had it finally arrived, the time referred to by all the critics (the author included) as "only then . . ."? Unfortunately not. A puzzling situation: almost all the conditions have been met, almost all the changes have been positive, and yet the end result is negative and counterproductive. Table 4 shows the problem.

Economist M. Lemeshev has analyzed the record of Gorbachev's so-called acceleration period, from 1986 to 1988. During that time, the GNP increased by 8.5 percent while waste of natural resources, rate of pollution, and destruction of

Table 4

Environmental Pollution in the USSR

Pollution and waste	1985	1988	Ratio of 1988 to 1985 (in %)
Dumping of sewage (bln. cub. m)	15.99	50.6	180
Sewage dumped (mln. cub. m)			
Baikal basin	124	191	154
Ladoga basin (Leningrad area)	271	392	145
Waste of natural gas in extraction and transportation (bln. cub. m)	12.9	15.1	117
Eroded plowland (mln. hec.)	133	218	164

Source: Environmental Protection and Rational Use of Natural Resources (Moscow: Goskomstat, 1989), pp. 94, 133, 135, 142.

the environment soared anywhere from 16 to 80 percent. According to Lemeshev, both extraction of raw materials and self-destructive industrial production increased. The government increased the budget for environmental protection from 2.5 billion rubles in 1985 to 3.1 billion in 1988, and the estimated average annual rate of government and industrial spending amounted to 10–11 billion rubles. Meanwhile, the cost of direct damage to the environment and public health has been put at 45–50 billion rubles per year.[3] Here is how Lemeshev explained the dilemma:

> There is a widely held view that the existing budgets for environmental protection are not enough, and an increase in these sums would bring about an improvement in the country's ecological situation. This way of thinking is fundamentally wrong. Given the extensive growth in production, based on resource-consuming "dirty" technologies, the objective of environmental protection is unattainable in principle, no matter how large the resources allocated for environmental measures. Moreover, without changing the structure of social production, without reducing the extraction of natural

resources, the increase in labor cost to preserve the environment will cause nothing but growing damage to the national economy and social welfare.[4]

In the last years of the Soviet regime the situation continued to deteriorate. There was a 400 percent increase in the amount of unprocessed sewage dumped into the Volga, and 300 percent more for the Azov Sea. Even the Baikal basin, despite the special project undertaken to protect its environment, received 150 percent more sewage.[5]

Despite the increasing amounts spent on programs for environmental protection, the damage to the environment and public health mounted quickly and inexorably.

Until 1986, experienced Soviet specialists could predict how badly and how soon the situation would deteriorate in area X or Y by the number of government decisions to improve conditions, increase productivity, and so forth in the given area. The attention of the authorities served as a reliable indicator that things were taking a turn for the worse. Ordinarily the country's leaders let a situation take its own course, so that whatever was bad got progressively worse. Nobody could stop it. An increasing number of resolutions only meant that a particular area was deteriorating more rapidly than the others.

Under Gorbachev the situation changed. Government decisions, at least where ecology was concerned, were based on open analysis. They say the truth is not always pleasant, but it pays. Soviet ecological policy disproved that rule, for despite the government's truthful statements and earnest resolutions, matters got increasingly worse. Here are some preliminary estimates of the total damage caused by environmental degradation in the USSR: for 1988, 45–50 billion rubles; for 1989, 90 billion rubles; for 1991, approximately 600 billion rubles. In 1990 two economists projected damage to public health at 400–450 billion rubles per year—over 66 percent of the GNP.[6]

In April 1990, speaking on television, N. Vorontsov admitted that the situation was sharply worsening, and it was time to "move from headlong deterioration to slow improvement." Vorontsov believed that increasing budgets and modernizing treatment facilities would help improve the situation. And indeed, after 1988 there were increases for an entire range of programs, from treatment facilities to forest planting. Yet it appears that Lemeshev was right: the money was of little avail.

In 1988 the Soviet Union only used about 65 percent of the overall funds allocated for water and air treatment facilities. Breaking down the figures, the Baltic republics used 80 percent or more, while the republics of Central Asia plus Azerbaijan and Georgia used as little as 1–5 percent of their budgets.[7]

Local governments have been encouraged to raise their own revenues to supplement or replace state funding. One potentially large source of revenue is, of course, the sale or development of natural resources, which means there is a strong incentive to exploit rather than conserve resources. In a pilot project during the late 1980s, the central authorities began charging many industries for water use. Consumption by industry naturally fell, so much so that the revenues of water agencies were reduced. In response, local authorities began to pressure industries to increase water consumption.

In Kemerovo, a Siberian town with extremely severe air pollution, ecological funding was not only increased, but Moscow gave the local authorities free rein to use the money at their own discretion. The result? After 1989 the town put an almost complete stop to construction of new facilities.[8]

As a matter of fact, for decades neither the USSR nor Czechoslovakia, Poland, and other socialist countries made full use of their environmental budgets. The average figures for budget utilization varied from 85 to 95 percent. These countries were viewed with irony as the only ones in the world that "overallocated" money for environmental protection while all the others were constantly scrambling for means to supplement their insufficient budgets.

This situation lasted for many years, but more recently, the change has been drastic. In the past, industrial and agricultural output, though floundering, still grew. In 1988–89 the USSR's economic output increased by a slight margin; at the end of 1990 came perceptible decline. By the first quarter of 1991, various estimates pointed at a 20–40 percent decrease in production.[9] This tendency has continued through 1992 and into 1993.

A similar situation existed in Poland in the early 1980s. At that time, Poland's industrial output suffered a sharp decline, yet there was an increase in the air and water pollution and the amount of waste produced. Despite the economic crisis, the Polish government continued to raise the environmental budgets— *and yet pollution steadily increased.* This was explained by political stagnation and the absence of democratic economic reforms.[10] Indeed, as soon as Poland embarked on the road of political reform, the state of its environment began to show signs of positive, though insignificant, changes.

But the situation in the USSR was not analogous. There, political changes directly concerned with the environment were set in motion in 1986, with the cancellation of a project to divert water from Siberia to Central Asia, and reached a peak in 1989. During the elections to the Supreme Soviet, and at the First Congress of People's Deputies in June 1989, nearly 90 percent of all the deputies, in their speeches or programs, demanded urgent laws, drastic measures, and emergency budgets aimed at saving the environment. Has the history of Western democracies seen anything approaching such concentrated public resolve to combat a single problem in peacetime?

It could not be said that "the voice of the people" was completely unheeded. Yet at the next congress, in December 1989, priorities were reversed: only 10 percent of the speakers raised ecological issues while the other 90 percent skirted them. Only two months later, at the Third Congress, held in February 1990, the "ecological lobby" shrank to a mere 5 percent of all the speakers.

The deputies' conduct had a logic of its own: the collapsing economy and ethnic conflicts verging on civil war claimed all of their attention. If politics is the art of the possible, the Supreme

Soviet deputies must have simply reached the conclusion that the task of stabilizing and revitalizing the environment was not feasible under the prevailing conditions.

Thus, Russian reality once again defies all credibility with its paradoxical and pathological oscillations. Ecological budgets grew, industrial production (including the "dirty" kind) went down, political reforms and Green activity intensified significantly —and still pollution continued to rise. What causes this chronic ailment and what can be done to alleviate the situation?

Deputy Andreev of USSR Prosecutor General's office pointed out that the level of pollution in the Volga started to rise precisely when the Society to Save the Volga came into existence. This occurred at the time when the authorities were doing nothing to prevent the Greens from widening their activity in every area—from ecological education to rallies protesting the construction of new atomic power stations. Furthermore, it was in that very period, when the government had finally passed a number of important laws and resolutions on environmental protection, that the curve of ecological crimes sharply rose.[11]

In Andreev's opinion, the average Soviet citizen's distorted morality was such that he was ready to spend more effort in bypassing and violating the law than in observing it. Thus, violations became the norm.

Valentin Rasputin, the writer who for many years fought to save the Baikal, received letters in which angry readers would ask him: "The Volga has been destroyed, along with the Dnieper, the Danube, and Lake Ladoga—so why should your Baikal stay clean? Forget it."[12]

It seems that the worse the situation got, the more people tended to blame laws and regulations and choose to disobey them. New laws could be passed; special ecological prosecutor's offices could even be created, as was being done throughout Russia. Yet the old system of prohibitions and punishments had lost its efficacy. There was an alternative—the type of property sanctions that are more or less efficiently applied in the West. But, leaving aside the question of weak legal norms, the people have no private property. Without private ownership, concluded Andreev in 1990, the country would be in irreparable trouble within two to three years' time. Now we are in 1993. . .

The Northern Front and the Energy Problem. The North is advancing south; the South is pushing north. The two eco-domino movements influence the European part of the former USSR. As we have seen, in the North the collapse of ecosystems is mainly related to the developing oil and gas industry and other types of mining on the one hand, and the extreme instability of northern ecosystems on the other. These systems are unlikely to become stronger and more stable. The positive changes that are supposed to be in store for the North as a consequence of the greenhouse effect, such as the movement of forests and productive agricultural lands closer to the Arctic circle, remain on paper as rosy and ungrounded projections while the opposite is taking place in reality.

Since the prime cause of the northern eco-domino is energy production, it is necessary to examine the trends in the development of the Soviet power industry. For the majority of the world's countries, raising energy consumption remains the most obvious and effective tool of economic growth. The classic common factor of development is that the growth of GNP requires an almost proportionate growth in energy consumption.

Soviet experts Makarov and Bashmakov analyzed seven different scenarios for developing a country's economy from the standpoint of minimizing emission of greenhouse gases. The Soviet Union, of course, was the world's second biggest producer of these emissions, after the United States. The future dynamics of these emissions could either speed up or slow down the warming process throughout the globe. Yet, as Makarov and Bashmakov pointed out, in any, even the most optimistic scenario, the former USSR would exhaust its quota of gas emissions for the period until the year 2100 as early as 2015, or at the most 2028.[13] According to the conclusions reached by Makarov and Bashmakov, it would be possible to reduce emissions by 15–16 percent over the next 20 years, provided there was an accelerated change in economic structures.[14]

Is it possible to cause a significant reduction in emissions from the burning of organic fuel? There are two ways: rapid development of energy-saving technologies, and rapid development of nuclear energy.

New nuclear power stations after Chernobyl? This option does not seem very feasible, at least for the next 10 to 20 years, possibly for good. Thus, what remains are the ecologically friendly techniques of power production, coupled with economic and efficient ways of using energy. This scenario promises a future reduction of gas emissions by 10 percent. It was for this reason that Soviet and Western Greens enthusiastically urged the start of an "energy revolution," whereby the USSR would be supplied with or sold the necessary facilities on favorable terms. Yet energy-saving technologies cost up to twice as much as the traditional methods of increasing power production. On the scale of the Soviet Union—for that is the scale required to achieve the 10 percent reduction—this means tens of billions of dollars over the next few years. The Soviet economy could never bear such a burden, and to date, there is no evidence of alternative sources of funding.[15]

Besides the financing, note should be made of the problem of efficient use of Western technology under Soviet conditions. After all, the existing facilities already are often left idle, or only partly used because of economic, social, and a host of other reasons.

From the point of view of the issue that concerns us at present—the stability of the European part of the former USSR—the conclusions of Makarov and Bashmakov mean that in the next decades the demand for energy is unlikely to undergo significant changes. Therefore, the country must continue to rapidly develop its energy resources in both the North and the South.[16]

Our subject and conclusions are quite definite: a reduction in energy consumption and production in the former USSR is an unrealistic goal. The country's European part, with 65 percent of the overall population and industrial output, is the main consumer of energy produced in the North. The extraction of oil, gas, and coal in Western Siberia and other northern areas causes further deterioration of the environment (which means further advance of the northern front toward the center of European Russia). After that, nearly 90 percent of the energy resources are shipped to the European region, where their burning inevitably pollutes the environment, weakening the ecosystems from within. Ultimately, the two sides of the energy coin—extraction and consumption—cause an acceleration in the eco-domino process threatening the entire European part of the former USSR.

The powerful impact of the collapsed northern ecosystems on the region situated in the south and west is significant due to the vast size of the tundra and coniferous taiga areas. Within the geographical borders of the European part of the country, these two zones occupy over one million square kilometers, or more than 15 percent of Soviet territory west of the Urals. Moreover, between these mountains and central Russia there are no mountain chains to serve as a natural buffer zone against the onslaught of the eco-domino process.

The eco-domino is offset by only one, albeit quite influential, factor: in the European part, the area of permafrost is rather narrow. Even in the tundra, not to mention the taiga, it does not form a solid line. As a result, the ecosystems are more stable, deteriorating less rapidly; correspondingly, the eco-domino process develops at a much weaker pace. To this day, the "patches" of eco-domino process in the European North, even up near Vorkuta, are measured in dozens of kilometers across, and not in hundreds of kilometers as in the Siberian tundra and taiga at approximately the same latitudes. The current situation is changing too quickly to allow any definite forecasts. In any case, however, the belt of taiga forests (and former forests) to the south of the Arkhangel'sk region and the Komi, as well the northern part of today's Viatka and Perm' regions, if it does not halt, at least it does not speed up the advance of the "northern front" of the eco-domino to the south and west.

Chernobyl, while giving birth to eco-glasnost, did more harm than good to the Soviet power industry: a wave of protests by the

Greens caused the authorities, from 1986 onward, to halt construction and shut down power stations capable of supplying no less than half of the energy currently consumed by the European part of the country. Most of the halted projects were nuclear power stations, but there were also some ordinary thermal power stations.[17]

A sprawling and conservative economy is incapable of rapid change and flexibility. For instance, in the Western countries the freezing of atomic projects had no tangible effect on the consumer, for there, reserve output represents 35–50 percent of the overall production, while in the USSR it was a mere 4–5 percent. It is no wonder that a hundred Soviet cities experienced a severe shortage of power in recent winters. What will happen next winter, with oil workers and miners going on longer strikes, ethnic conflicts, and republics "closing the valves" on gas pipelines and energy exchange? Rational and humanitarian considerations have less and less weight. Total and sudden shutdowns happen not only to hundreds of factories but also to hospitals and homes for the disabled as, for example, during the conflict between Georgia and Northern Ossetia.[18]

In reality, economic and technological considerations, not to mention the psychological factor, require increasing amounts of energy to be produced, and produced today. The role of psychology must not be underestimated. Russia today is not just a country with traditionally low living standards—it is a country in the advanced stages of collapse. The difference is that the collapsing society has seen better days, a more orderly economy, and slowly but definitely improving living standards. Today that society is angry and irritable, and the public mood plays an even more decisive role than economic or technological factors.

If Soviet and Western experts once reached a reasonable mutual understanding about the greenhouse effect, the same cannot be said about the problem of living standards. It is hard to imagine the global consequences if economic reform were to lead to the same rate of energy consumption in Russia as in the West.

Robert Sokolov, a professor at Princeton University who is an expert in power engineering, has cautioned against the risks of spreading America's living standards throughout the entire world. If Russia and China had the same number of cars, refrigerators, and washing machines per capita as the United States, the world would face ecological collapse.

"I must say," objected economist M. Lemeshev, "that this is a very strange logic—placing limitations on raising the living standards for all the countries except the United States, as a way to protect the environment."[19]

The focal point of disagreement is, of course, the car—a car for every family. "The dream of a cottage in the country with a double garage has no future," says Sandra Postel of the independent Washington-based Worldwatch Institute. The same idea has been voiced by dozens of specialists throughout the Western world. However, here is the reaction of the Russian ecologist Iaroshenko:

> We already tried to build Communism in one country, and it didn't work. It would be even less realistic to build an ecological heaven in that same country, producing semifinished goods for others while the rest of the world consumes the products of civilization. . . . Cars are the one thing desired by millions; and they are capable of uniting the country and lending mobility to the labor force—the very thing we need. . . .

Iaroshenko continues:

> Of course, the world will achieve an ecological culture, ecological economy, balanced development, alternative sources of power, waste-free technologies, electrical and sun-powered cars, industrial growth limited by international conventions. But this will not be achieved at once or by isolated countries. Right now we are living in a huge country, sunk in impassable roads, deprived of normal modern communications. We must raise it to the level of civilized dignity; then, and only then, can we conduct mutual discussions about a worldwide network of ecological protection. . . .

Today the theme of global ecological safety is orchestrated by Western egotism. The West is disturbed over the expected warming of the global climate. Yet it is unwilling to pay according to its contribution to the deterioration of natural environment, unwilling to share its latest technology.[20]

In other words, the West is saying: Avoid repeating our mistakes. Look for alternative paths of development, or else we will all die out, burn to cinders, fall into the inferno.

All right, the East bluntly replies, since we are heading for hell anyway, we prefer to drive there, like you. If the dream of having a double garage really has no future, let that apply to everyone. The fact that you already have a house in the country does not mean that it could not be torn down, starting with the garage.

Dostoevsky's observation that the Russian peasant would rather have a prosperous neighbor brought down to his own level of squalor than strive to live as well as his neighbor can explain a good deal in Russian history. Berdiaev used this idea as one of the basic points in his explanation of the origins and meaning of Russian communism. It seems that the ecologist Iaroshenko gives expression to that same fervent, unquenchable thirst for equality—this time on the ecological plane, on the level of biological survival, and on the global scale.

Of course, Russia has no cause to strike the attitude of being "humiliated and downtrodden" by the West (rather the contrary). In reality, four-fifths of the world live under even worse conditions than the Russians. At the same time, anyone who follows developments in Russia must surrender any illusion that calls for a rational approach to persuade people who are experiencing unprecedented poverty and despair.[21]

For that very reason, no one should place illusory hopes on Russian cooperation in the field of environmental protection in general, and energy-related policies in particular, without some tangible compromise on the part of the West. By tangible compromise I mean economic sacrifices, a lowering of living standards, including a reduction in the number of cars. Freezing

Western living standards at their present level would not be enough; the gap would still be shockingly great. To be sure, neither should there be any illusions as to the West's willingness to lower its living standards—but that is another subject.

The Southern Front and Destabilization of the Human Habitat. The eco-domino is not moving systematically toward a specific end point. Desertification and other types of ecosystem collapse always expand at the expense of less stable, more weakened ecosystems, regardless of where they are situated.

At the same time, it is highly important that European Russia is feeling the simultaneous impact of two fronts at once—the northern and the southern. If the advance of the northern front, as we have already seen, is related primarily to the reckless exploitation of energy resources, in the south the prime cause is desertification, mainly of agricultural origins. To be sure, here too the shortage of energy contributes its destructive share, leaving no chances for halting or even minimizing the devastating impact of development of the Tengiz and Astrakhan regions.

The dynamics of the eco-domino must be examined not only in terms of offensive factors (the intensity of the sources of deterioration and the already deteriorated area), but also in terms of the defensive capabilities of a given area. No less important than the potential for expansion is the potential for resisting expansion; both the eco-domino's origins and its destination must be taken into account.

Due to a number of natural factors, the European part is considerably more stable than any other region of the former USSR (primarily since it is in a temperate forest zone, abundant in water, with a flat plain occupying most of its surface.) However, the southern steppes—from southern Ukraine to the lower Volga—have always suffered from aridity, and are potentially more susceptible to desertification. The area could not be expected to function as a buffer zone of the type that could possibly be formed by the forests of the Arkhangel'sk region, the Komi, and other areas in the north of Russia. This is amply demonstrated by the situation in Kalmykia. Meanwhile, the state of the Caspian, Azov, and Black seas serves as a reliable indicator of the troubles plaguing their basins.

"If twenty years ago," writes M. Lemeshev, "destruction of nature had a largely local character,"

> . . . we are now witnessing the formation of vast ecological disaster areas which not only destroy nature but pose a threat to the health and life itself of millions of people. These include vast areas of Central Russia, the Lower Volga, the basins of the Caspian and Azov seas, . . . Southern Ukraine, the areas around the Chernobyl disaster, resorts of the Caucasus and the Crimea, the Riga coast. . . . There is ever-increasing water and air pollution, deforestation, destruction of land, with the accompanying deterioration of human society.[22]

In the European part of the country, what causes the greatest alarm among ecologists is the tendency of disaster areas to expand by pushing at the adjoining, relatively stable areas, and the merging of the "patches" and enclaves of ecological disaster to form large territorial blocks. This is especially obvious in the Volga basin, where over the past few years separate parts of the middle and lower Volga have actually formed one solid ecological disaster area.

The gravity of the situation is apparent in the map of ecological disaster areas created by the Institute of Geography of the USSR Academy of Sciences. Based on considerable research, the map locates 291 destabilized areas whose inhabitants face serious health problems related to various types of pollution. These areas comprised approximately 16–21 percent of the entire Soviet territory.[23] At first glance, this figure may not seem all that ominous; however, it should be stressed that it refers to the entire area of this huge country. If we were to project the data onto the European scale, the disaster areas may be said to have enveloped an area larger than all of Western Europe including Scandinavia—a total of 3.6–4 million kilometers.

In the European part of the former USSR, which is the most densely populated, about one-half of the area appears to fall under the category of ecological disaster. This includes deforested and no longer arable lands, vast stretches of eroded and polluted soil, as well as areas where natural resources are extracted and put to industrial use. In addition to areas of extreme ecological danger, the map indicates areas affected by acid rain—a further 10–12 percent of the territory in the European part of the country. Like their Western counterparts, Russian experts give priority to the perils of soil contamination as a basic denominator of environmental stability. In order to make an accurate estimate of an ecosystem's stability, one should take into account the fact that areas strongly affected by acid rain are adjacent to areas of ecological disaster and constitute the focal point of their potential expansion. For instance, on the Kola Peninsula and in the area around St. Petersburg, it is hard to find "normal" ecosystems; almost all of them are classified as disaster areas or areas suffering from heavy acid rain. Ecological disasters are everywhere—"to the south and the north, the east and the west of a country that seems to be suffering the aftereffects of a chemical or a geophysical war," in the words of geographer V. Kotliakov.[24]

The Baltic countries and Belarus are in a relatively better position. However, the map does not include the effects of radiation from the Chernobyl disaster. As noted by Soviet and Western researchers, this radiation is affecting several million people in Belarus and Ukraine, with the contaminated area constantly expanding due to the radioactive fallout carried through the air. Maps published in the USSR invariably show an ever-increasing number of new contaminated areas far to the east and south of the previous ones. Radiation has spread (or has it been there ever since the disaster?) as far as the south of the Moscow region.

It is even more difficult to halt the spread of radiation in surface and groundwater. Today, most water reservoirs in the Dnieper basin are still within the permissible limits for radioactivity, but highly radioactive soil particles gradually accumulate at the bottom of these reservoirs. This process is irreversible. Some experts predict that over the next ten to fifteen years, tens of millions of local residents will be seriously damaged by the effects of radiation in the sources of water.[25]

It is important to note the distinct geographical features of the Chernobyl disaster zone. The contaminated area was more stable ecologically than other areas of the European part of the USSR. Northern Ukraine and Belarus are many hundreds of kilometers to the west of the badly polluted Volga area, and only a little closer to the heavily industrialized disaster area of the Donbass and southern Ukraine. This used to be a sort of "clearing," a land mass in the center of the European part of the USSR, somewhat affected by acid rains. Today a major portion of this land is contaminated by radiation. That is why the long-term consequences of Chernobyl far outweigh the mere addition of a few hundred square kilometers to the total area of environmental disaster.

Radiation is a particular kind of environmental pollution, and I do not possess the criteria for evaluating stability of ecosystems according to radiation levels. It is known that the damage caused by radioactive substances emerges only after a long period of time; the surface soil may even show signs of increasing fertility and biomass production. Nevertheless, from the point of view of human survival and economic value, these regions should be categorized as extremely destabilized ecological areas, though of a different type of destabilization.

It has been estimated that as many as 17 million people may fall victim to radiation in the former USSR and Eastern Europe.[26] The latest reports by Soviet specialists stated that medical damage caused by the accident in Belarus had reached alarming proportions. The number of thyroid problems had doubled in southern Belarus; cases of anemia in the fallout zone had increased by 700–800 percent; chronic disorders of the nasopharynx had increased tenfold; the incidence of blood and liver disorders among small children had risen; there was a substantial increase in cases of cataracts, as well as leukemia and other types of cancers, especially among children.[27]

Only five years after the catastrophe were Soviet specialists able to estimate the effects of small and accumulating dosages of radiation on human genetics. Even the official data are more than disturbing. Suffice it to say that in Belarus genetic disorders are reported to have risen by 15 to 20 percent as compared to the period before 1986. (Unofficial estimates put the figure at 25 percent.)[28] The 15–25 percent rise in genetic disorders, observed in the first generation only, when combined with the data cited above, shifts the problem onto a different level altogether. After Chernobyl, the discussion should focus not only on unstable ecosystems, but also on the instability of the human population in the area. What do we mean by instability of the population?

Health problems arising as a result of environmental pollution and destruction receive the greatest attention of Soviet specialists and the press. For the average Soviet, the notion of environmental protection meant, above all, preservation of physical and mental health. This emphasis differentiated the Soviet approach from the concept of environmental protection widely accepted in the West, which focuses on humankind's natural surroundings.

According to a report by the Ecology Committee of the USSR Supreme Soviet, about 80 percent of the country's total illness rate was directly or indirectly related to environmental pollution, noise, and other ecological factors. The committee reported that the country's population had an average life expectancy of 69 years; an infant mortality rate (up to 1 year) of 24.7 per 1,000; a 1–4 percent annual increase in the number of oncological patients; and statistics showing that 23 percent of children under age seven and 14 percent of high-school students were healthy, while 20 percent of schoolchildren suffered from allergies.

The USSR Ministry of Public Health analyzed public health figures for 184 Soviet cities with a high level of industrial pollution. The results showed that excessive concentration of at least one pollutant led to a 70 percent increase in sickness rates (for some age-groups the figure is as high as 300 percent).[29]

The summary that follows is from the work of G. Sidorenko, a famous public health expert.

Even if environmental pollution were to be totally eliminated in the near future (which is absolutely unrealistic), this would not prevent a further increase in diseases such as malignant tumors caused by delayed effects of environmental factors, primarily chemical agents with latent activity span of twenty to fifty years. It is precisely the delayed effects of pollution (carcinogenic, mutagenous, embriotoxic, disruption in gonad functioning, etc.) that cause the most alarm at present. By now it has been firmly determined that an entire series of chemical substances have carcinogenic and/or mutagenous effects in the concentrations in which they are present in the environment in many areas throughout the country. A crucial negative effect is contributed by the chemical industry, which manufactures hundreds of new compounds with unknown properties. A couple of years ago, when red snow fell in the area of Derbenevskii Quay in Moscow, even the experts did not know exactly what the substance was or how it got into the air. Only when disturbing symptoms manifest themselves do they begin to be studied. However, the effects often have a prolonged delayed action, and are discovered too late, when health has been damaged beyond repair.

Especially dangerous, in the sense of delayed consequences, is the mutagenous effect of pollution. Since the late 1960s, the USSR has experienced a significant rise in the rate of congenital defects among the newborn. The most polluted areas of human habitat are accumulating a "genetic load" with totally unpredictable consequences for future generations.

The lead content in the bodies of middle-aged people is presently twenty times as high as it was a hundred years ago. The fatty tissue among a portion of the population in various regions has been discovered to contain a high concentration of chlororganic compounds—DDT and PCB. Although these concentrations have not yet reached critical levels, the same harmful properties are contained in mercury, cadmium, silver, and other heavy metals, while the combined effect of various chemical compounds on the human organism may increase.

Finally, hygiene studies have reported a decline in the immune resistance among the larger portion of the population. An increasing percentage of the population are defined as high-risk groups, liable to develop both specific and nonspecific pathological disorders.

Chemical and biological environmental pollution costs the country annual losses of millions of man-years and billions of rubles. This is the truth that we must face.[30]

We must face the truth, including the fact that in the near future, as I have already pointed out, the damage incurred because of premature loss of lives, health, and work efficiency will claim up to three-quarters of GNP. Of course, as is often pointed out, Russia is an enormous country. Some areas must be better off than others.

I suggest that we consider Moscow as the best sample. As the capital, Moscow has always been better off than the rest of the country in every area of life; in any case, it is no worse than the Russian average. Moscow is also a logical example from the point of view of geography, since we are interested in measuring the stability of the European part of the former USSR, and Moscow is at its heart.

There is an additional consideration—of a sentimental nature—for using Moscow: it was the first place where serious thought was given to the deadly effect of pollution on human health.

Moscow as a Sample. Today it is California that is recognized as the world leader in many fields of ecology. In Los Angeles, "the birthplace of smog," the most complex—and costly—research is being carried out, on the basis of which the state sets its standards for water and air pollution and food contamination. Analogous standards are adopted in turn by other American states, Canada, Sweden, Denmark, the Netherlands, and other developed countries, and, finally, by Eastern Europe, the former Soviet states, and parts of the Third World. This pattern reflects the degrees of flexibility of various governments as well as the extent of public concern over the environmental threat in a given country. Nowadays, proximity to California's standards may serve as an indicator of the strength of a country's ecological policies.

This was not always the case, however. There was a time when Moscow was doing the job carried out by California today. Professor John Goldsmith, an environmental epidemiologist who has been working in California for many years, once told me: "My serious work on pollution standards began with what I learned from the Russians. Academician Riazanov helped me more than any of my Western teachers."

There is an unconfirmed story that in 1942, virtually on the eve of the battle of Stalingrad, Stalin allocated funds for Riazanov to conduct research on safety standards for potable water.* In 1944 the Soviet leader signed a decree giving some fifty of Riazanov's norms the force of law. This was the world's first legislation on water purity. But after a noisy propaganda campaign, neither Stalin nor his ministers (nor any of their successors over the next thirty years) showed any further interest in the problem of water purity, and Riazanov's standards were never implemented.

Yet it would be wrong to say that Riazanov's standards served no other cause than Stalin's propaganda. Even if only on paper, they have proved of value; his methods have been used by specialists throughout the world to set similar norms.

By the mid-1950s Riazanov had also worked out standards for air pollution. The bureaucratic rigmarole required to enact these standards into law demanded enormous efforts. Riazanov was dead of heart attack when the call came through to inform him of the government's positive decision.

The Institute of General and Communal Hygiene continues to function in Moscow today, employing a number of specialists of the Riazanov school. However, anyone who has listened to their opinions on current ecological problems would think twice before drinking a drop of tap water or taking a bite out of a lettuce leaf bought in Moscow. Breathing, of course, is not a matter of choice, but of black humor: "It's okay to breathe but not to inhale."

---

*I personally doubt that Stalin could have initiated such a measure. However, I know of an actual case when in 1942 he allotted money for making a film . . . on bees, called *The Sun-Tribe*. After the war the film was shown at numerous international festivals, including at Cannes, where it enjoyed enormous success for its unique subject matter. It is quite plausible that Stalin, with his excellent propaganda sense, ordered some official in his huge retinue to select humane subjects in science, art, and literature, lending support whenever it served his interests.

When the World Health Organization began to analyze statistical data for eighty of the world capitals, Moscow was found to rank sixty-second in the rate of births, seventy-first in population increase, and seventy-fifth in life expectancy. Moscow's average life expectancy is three to five years behind that of Vienna, Montreal, Paris, Stockholm, and Tokyo. It ranks sixty-fourth in the rate of surviving children. Eight percent of Moscow's children suffer from oligophrenia. Thirty-three percent of children under seven should be considered marginal, while by age seventeen their number increases to 45 percent.[31] From 1977 to 1985 the number of children suffering from asthma increased by 750 percent. Among school-age children, 70–75 percent are unhealthy, and new types of multiple allergy disorders have appeared. Why? It seems likely that increased pollution levels are one of the major reasons for this rise in health problems.

According to official reports, since 1986 a number of radioactive dumps from the 1950s and 1960s have been neutralized. Yet the reports failed to specify their number, or how many are still left. Moscow Greens reported that three sites with high radioactivity had been discovered in new residential developments. The authorities knew about one of them, and halted the construction of an apartment building on the site. It was built instead on an adjacent site; eventually, the residents began to use the empty lot as a playground for their children.[32]

Of all the pollution problems in the Russian capital, soil contamination from cadmium, lead, and mercury has received the most study. However, in this instance knowledge does not bring good news. Scholars working for the Ministry of Geology compiled a special map on which areas where the concentration of those metals exceeds safety standards by as much as fifteen, twenty, forty, or even sixty times are marked in varying shades of red. Airborne dust particles also contain dangerous concentrations of these substances. Indeed, the sand in some children's playgrounds is so highly contaminated that one expert has recommended erecting notices there marked "Danger! Poison."

It is not surprising that the "red" areas on the map exactly coincide with the regions where sickness rates are the highest. Even now, there is no modern system of neutralizing toxic industrial waste in Moscow. Every year, for example, some 10 million fluorescent light bulbs containing mercury are simply discarded on dumps. Part of the mercury evaporates, and another part is absorbed into the soil and the underground water system. The "Mad Hatter's disease" and "Minamata disease" (two forms of mercury poisoning) have been reported in the press, but no details have been given.[33]

The land farmed by kolkhozes in the vicinity of Moscow is also in a wretched condition. This is mainly because, over a long period of time, the soil has been fertilized with organic sediment accumulated by the city's sewage purification plants. Specialists warn that these deposits contain many heavy metals originating from industrial enterprises. No systematic research into this problem has been carried out; however, from a runoff test in the River Istra region, it was discovered that the soil of entire farms contained unacceptable quantities of cadmium, lead, and zinc. This gives rise to speculations concerning the situation in other collective farms as well as the private plots where peasants grow carrots, lettuce, radishes, and cabbages that are later sold in Moscow markets. No one is in the position to answer this question. Nevertheless, studies carried out by Polish ecologists who have encountered the same problem in Silesia demonstrated that cabbages grown on land with a high concentration of cadmium appear fresher and more appetizing than usual, and are invariably preferred by market shoppers.[34]

Early in 1990 I presented a Moscow acquaintance of mine with a portable filter capable of obtaining drinking water out of virtually any liquid, be it water from the Red Sea, milk, or orange juice. Some time later, she used the filter to check the water from an ordinary house tap, and the results of her test were reported in a newspaper article.

> Such clean, delicious, cool water! Yet twenty seconds later the red light was blinking: Stop! Danger to life! The sight was so absurd that

I was sure it must be a mistake, a defective sample that has far outlived its fitness date, a phony gift from a tight-fisted foreigner. . . .

A few years ago (at the very height of Prohibition) all the Moscow papers vied with each other in ridiculing American reporters who had arrived in the capital to cover a top-level meeting, while carrying suitcases filled with . . . drinking water in plastic bottles. Today, some years later, having lived through the Ufa and Barnaul disasters as well as scores of other water accidents of a smaller scale, we seem to have become more tolerant of others' customs, and more cautious in our own self-appraisal.

In the center of Russia, at Staryi Izborsk by the Slav Springs, a group of bicyclists appear each morning, carrying iron canisters on their racks. They are Pskov and Pechora monks, changed into civilian clothes, who come for ice-cold spring water from almost twenty kilometers away, from the almost pollution-free Pechory.

After Moscow tap water, I too enjoyed a taste of the Izborsk spring water. Suddenly, a splitting headache, quickened heart beat— clear signs of poisoning. But can one get poisoning from clear water? Then I remembered—the bird market, and the Sunday winos at the entrance, selling jars with multicolored guppies at the unbelievably low price of fifty for a ruble. The experienced fish fancier knows that these little fish are caught in the Liubertsy cesspools. A rookie, however, might just buy them, not knowing that at home all fifty would leap out of the aquarium and die within seconds. These are mutant fish, with odd-looking tails and gills, whose sole ecological niche is the cesspool; any other place, anything living, is deadly.

On the average, every Muscovite uses some 600 liters of water per day; the analogous figure for Londoners is 250 liters. However, it would be rash to conclude that the residents of Moscow are cleaner than those in London, or that drinking water poses no problem in the Russian capital. The discrepancy in numbers can be explained simply by the fact that the Moscow plumbing system works on the principle of quantity above quality. There is a widely held view that all information on water is kept secret in our country. Alexander Lopatin, Chief Supervisor of Moscow water supplies, explained that there are no secrets concerning water—not because there is no mystery, but rather because there is nothing to make a mystery out of:

There are no data, because there is a shortage of equipment, techniques, chemicals, and, of course, hard currency with which all of those things could be purchased abroad. True, foreign embassies in Moscow have express labs on their premises, capable of detecting up to 300 "alien presences" in water within minutes. But those are others' secrets, not ours. As to our own central laboratory, its director has explained that it is within her competence to say yes or no for no more than ten elements.[35]

The Kremlin bosses, of course, no longer drink tap water. Nonetheless, the former total insulation of the Soviet ruling class from the environment does seem to have come to an end, not only in the figurative but also in the literal sense.

One of the reasons Moscow was allowed to become so polluted was that the political elite enjoyed protection from a wide range of pollutants. Areas where Politburo members and other high-ranking officials reside—Kuntsevo, the Sparrow Hills, and Fili—used to be kept relatively clean. On the map of soil pollution, they are colored green, which signifies a comparatively low level of contamination. However, only a few kilometers away the concentration of toxic elements in the air is no longer low.

The elite has also been affected by food contamination. Starting in the 1960s, most of the food in "Central Committee" dining rooms and shops with restricted access was supplied by collective and state farms where virtually no pesticides, mineral fertilizers, and other similar substances were used. These were called "dietetic products." However, sturgeon and stellate sturgeon, which produce black caviar, cannot be bred in artificial conditions but only in their natural habitat—the lower reaches of the Volga—and they have been virtually wiped out by an unknown disease which was clearly linked to large-scale water pollution. When this sturgeon was fed to laboratory mice, they became sick. Their fur was tousled, their behavior changed, and their reproductive cells were later discovered to contain highly mutagenous substances.[36] Although no one could claim that in recent years the hair of the Moscow elite has become more "tousled" (their behavior is even harder to evaluate), consumption of

contaminated caviar and sturgeon could not have failed to increase the risk of various diseases and genetic disturbances
among frequent eaters. Clean and healthy sturgeon must have
been absent from the Volga and the Caspian for years, even
though we may assume that toxic levels were much lower a few
years back.

Black caviar and sturgeon have been more than a delicacy—
they have been Russia's symbol abroad. Still, if it was the last
sacrifice they had to make, in all probability Muscovites would
eventually become reconciled to the loss of black caviar. In recent years they have endured more humiliating blows to their
pride. But the problem goes deeper than that, and the example of
toxic black caviar leads to a more thorough understanding of the
predicament. Reproductive cells are biologically the best protected part of the organism, the last to be invaded by harmful
substances. Analogously, Moscow, and especially the elite resid-
ing in the capital, have been the best protected part of the
country's social organism (without dwelling, to be sure, on the
elite's intellectual and other qualities as a group). If things have
deteriorated to such an extent that ecological problems have pen-
etrated every barrier of the social organism, the situation is really
very bad.

Social Impact. There is a Russian saying that has become well
known because of the insight it provides into the Russian national spirit: "Until the thunder strikes, the muzhik will not cross
himself." The thunder has struck in Chernobyl, affecting 17 million people. Could there be thunder louder than that? I have been
shown two volumes of laws and resolutions adopted by the central and Ukrainian governments between 1986 and 1989 in the
wake of Chernobyl. None of these decisions has been fully implemented, and definitely none of them has led to the expected
improvements.

Thunder has also struck at the Aral Sea and in Fergana, where
vast parcels of land contain up to 2,000 times the permissible
levels of DDT.[37] It has struck on Sakhalin Island, where the

water near the resort beach contains 1,956 times more cadmium than the norm allows. The thunder has struck, and yet, as a headline in the Soviet ecological newspaper *Spasenie* has put it, no one is crossing himself. Either the act of crossing is not enough without faith, or there have been too many thunderclaps too close together.

I do not intend to draw generalizations based on one article or popular saying. However, there is a glaring contradiction that needs to be analyzed. On the one hand, ecological problems acquired top priority for the majority of Soviet citizens. This was evident in what seems to have been the first opinion poll of this kind in decades, conducted in the USSR at the end of 1989.[38] So there is no doubt that people are seriously concerned. The question is whether this concern finds any expression in active measures aimed at improving the situation.

I have analyzed 300 articles on ecology that were published in Soviet newspapers and magazines between 1989 and 1991, looking for evidence of popular attitude about pressing ecological issues. Social cynicism, apathy, or lack of faith were directly mentioned in sixty-three articles and indirectly reflected in another twenty. In other words, 25 percent of the articles dealt with these issues directly or indirectly. Only fifteen articles (5 percent) contained any information on improving the ecological situation locally. Fourteen articles mentioned an escalation in violence related to ecological protests.

What are the concrete manifestations of apathy? I have already mentioned the pathological stoicism displayed by mothers in the Aral area at the sight of their dying babies, a feeling of resignation explainable by the fact that the woman is often herself gravely ill and exhausted by her domestic responsibilities. Here are two additional examples.

The *Moscow News* reporter who had written an article on the Ural town of Karabash, where incidence of cancer is higher than in the area adjoining the Semipalatinsk nuclear test site (338 per year per 100,000 inhabitants), and where the authorities admitted that there were virtually no healthy children, was astonished less

Question: "Which problem is the most urgent in our society?"
1. Shortage of manufactured goods   55%
2. Shortage of foodstuffs   51%
3. Inequitable allocation of goods and services   49%
4. Environmental pollution   47%
5. High prices   47%
6. Shortage of housing   35%
7. Poor medical service   31%
8. Having to deal with red tape   27%
9. Inferior education system   24%
10. Inadequate care for senior citizens   23%

Respondents in the Moscow area ranked the problems as follows:
1. Shortage of housing   20%
2. Environmental pollution   19%
3. High prices   15%

Question: "Which problem is the most important for you personally?"
1. High prices   18%
2. Shortage of housing   17%
3. Environmental pollution   14%

Question: "What should be dealt with immediately, versus later?"
1. Environmental pollution   87%
2. Shortage of foodstuffs   82%
3. Shortage of housing   78%

Question: "What is the most important aspect of the ecology problem?"
1. Air pollution   69%
2. Water pollution   54%
3. Danger of radiation   42%

by the figures than by people's resignation and fatalistic attitude. "Where can we go? . . . Strikes? No. People would not support us, because they would not be paid their salaries."[39]

The Public Health Minister of Bashkiria, where the drinking water, contaminated for years, has caused a steep rise in cancer, infant mortality, and congenital abnormalities, appealed to enterprises and the public to contribute money for the purchase of medical equipment from the West. Unfortunately, the minister's repeated appeals evoked no public reaction.[40] There has been manifest apathy, which, however, according to the authors of the publication cited, may rapidly escalate into violence on any pretext, including ecological issues.

In the summer of 1989, roughly the time of the poll cited above, Academician N. Amosov, a well-known physician and commentator, conducted a sociological survey. The response to environmental questions reflected a less than active involvement on the part of the public. If the ecological disaster can be expected to strike in twenty years, roughly half of the public are willing to contribute 10 percent or more of their income; if not for fifty years, then only 25 percent of the respondents would agree to such a sacrifice. For children in their city, people are ready to sacrifice 1.5 percent of their income; for the country's children, up to 1.0 percent; for the children of Africa, 0.1 percent. The respondents justified these paltry figures by citing the destitute state of Soviet society.[41]

"We have millions of radiation victims, not only in Chernobyl but also in Semipalatinsk, Cheliabinsk, Novaia Zemlia," says Svet Zabelin, a biologist and a leading member of the Moscow Greens. "Not only our generation but their children—too many of them are doomed. . . . What are we supposed to do? Ignore them?"[42]

He is answered by the readers of *Family*, a relatively new magazine, founded since the advent of perestroika.

The editors' survey on the subject of "Society and Retarded Children" failed to generate wide public response, and the reason will become clear from what follows. Eighty percent of the respondents did not accept the solution of "just ignoring" retarded children; nor did they suggest that such children should be "not ignored." What these 80 percent believe is that *retarded children should be put to death*. I imagine that the full meaning of that phrase may not sink in right away, so I will reiterate: not institutionalized, not sterilized, but *killed*.

Here is another statistic that requires the reader's self-possession: *the overwhelming majority of the respondents were women*. One of them (a Russian-born resident of the Baltic region) suggested with unrepressed malice that homes for mentally retarded children should be burned down. "While our own children lack the basic necessities, these degenerates get free food, furniture, television sets."[43]

"When a people's spirit has been drained, its first choice among all the freedoms available to it will inevitably be the freedom of malevolence," said one Russian writer. Where does ecology end and morality start? Or where is the dividing line between geography and public health? The ecological crisis has merged them into one.

We should the face the facts. Today's Russia is in the grips of an environmental crisis that involves huge areas and has led to physical and psychological deterioration of the people inhabiting those areas. The authors of the map of environmental disaster areas express this in blunt terms when they speak of *the extinction of human population caused by environmental changes.*[44]

Today's Russia is a disintegrating society which is not only powerless to curb environmental disintegration but, on the contrary, effectively contributes to the headlong advance of the destruction.

It can hardly be claimed that today's West, East, South, or North possesses handy recipes for handling the economic crisis, let alone the political one. Still, at least some measure of experience has been accumulated in this area, above all the ability to diagnose the instability inherent in the situation. Here, at least, there is some knowledge of what to expect, and what, sooner or later, can be achieved. Ultimately, stabilization has been a matter of time, and, of course, of the price the destabilized society was prepared to pay.

There has never before been a case when a society's political and economic structures disintegrated along with its physical environment. This combination is unprecedented. We may be capable of appreciating the aggressive danger of such a combination —we seem to be imaginative enough to feel fear. But do we have enough time to learn the way to stop the approaching collapse?

6

The Westward Advance

The world may have become a global village, but the human mind still reduces it to human scale. A day's travel by car or train is still considered a large distance. How could events even farther away affect us? "Russia's troubles are too far away for me to worry about," thinks the average European, though he sees tangible proof that areas of ecological danger are expanding.

The collapse of the Berlin Wall has meant the joining of enormous Eastern areas to what has been considered as Europe proper, without suffixes and definitions. For Europe, the fall of the wall signifies the "end of geography" in the same sense that the end of the Cold War was said to symbolize the "end of history."

Political leaders often appeal to history in times of crisis, usually with phrases on the model "History leaves us no choice." Today I would replace the word "history" with "geography" or "ecology," for there is one type of integration that had spread throughout the European continent long before Gorbachev appeared —and that is ecological integration. The flows of pollution have been converging. So far, only one geographical aspect of pollution transfer has been given wide publicity. I refer to the transfer of air pollution, for example, from England and France, flowing eastward to cause acid rains in Sweden and Switzerland, which themselves emit relatively small amounts of pollution.

There are other flows of pollution in various directions: the Rhine and the Vistula carry polluted water northward, the Danube and the Dnieper carry it southward. The Baltic and the Black seas, polluted by "capitalists" and "communists" alike, have a significant effect on the North Sea and the Mediterranean. Then there is the mining industry on the Kola Peninsula, which sends Scandinavia more sulfurous gas than Sweden, Norway, and Finland put together.

Europe is no longer divided by the Berlin Wall. In the fall of 1990 Eduard Shevardnadze proposed in a speech at the United Nations the idea of a unified Eurasian entity, indivisible economically, ecologically, and technologically. Due credit should be given to those Soviet leaders who had the foresight to raise such questions while the European Community remained preoccupied with tariffs, financial systems, and production standards.

It was Chernobyl that forced Gorbachev, Shevardnadze, and some others to recognize that the horror and suffering caused by the ecological collapse would affect the Soviets first of all. However, the consequences will inevitably "overflow" national borders.

Russian leaders, in their requests for aid from the West, have grown increasingly blunt: "perestroika helped the world, now it is the world's turn to help us"; "by helping us, you will help yourselves." Without Western billions, they hint, the reins of the Russian troika, barely controllable as it is, will slacken altogether, and it will go galloping wildly over mountains and dales. This is a prospect to be feared not only by the Russian riders but by everyone in their vicinity, not to mention that of their nuclear missiles, atomic power stations, and other dangerous installations.

"Our country cannot be 'fenced off' and events allowed to take their own course," argued the reform economist G. Iavlinskii. "Not only because the USSR occupies one-sixth of the world's area. It also has the largest nuclear potential, as well as stores of chemical and biological weapons, dozens of atomic power stations, and scores of other industrial installations. With the escalating violence in the country, this cannot be ignored—the case of Chernobyl speaks too eloquently."[1]

The geographical unity of Eurasia means that the eco-domino process on Soviet territory constitutes a kind of expansion toward the Western countries. This eco-expansion has no "control center" that organizes and coordinates depletion of forests and extinction of wildlife, or water poisoning and land erosion. There are no religious fanatics or ideological zealots responsible for the acid rain and the propagation of algae that ruin the Mediterranean beaches. The "coordination" of destructive forces takes place on the level of biological factors. The enemy is not easy to identify, and is therefore difficult to combat.

Years ago, European specialists began to realize that Europe's ecological stability in the coming decades would largely depend on factors that were virtually beyond their control. These included the greenhouse effect, climatic changes, rising sea level, depletion of the ozone layer, and destruction of tropical forests. Pattern studies, which included evaluation of the ecological situation based on ten separate parameters, predict a moderately serious to very serious deterioration if the world fails to shift to the so-called environmentally friendly path of development. As the researchers concluded, "the next generation of Europeans will be the first for whom environmental quality in Europe will depend largely on *human activities generated outside Europe*." Even if Western Europe curbs its economic growth, and makes every effort to save its environment, in such crucial parameters as sea level, water management, and forestry wood supply, it will find itself on the brink of disaster by the year 2030. In another four parameters, the situation will deteriorate markedly. Only in respect to three indicators can West Europeans be said to keep their foot on the brake of the environmental vehicle: these are soil acidification, pollution of coastal regions, and nonpoint toxins.[2]

However, the destabilizing impact of neighboring Eastern Europe and the former Soviet Union has not been taken into serious account due to insufficient data and the general vagueness of the situation. And, of course, the effect of the ecological deterioration of Eastern Europe and the former USSR on Western Europe influences the form and magnitude of global climatic changes as well. Yet the eco-domino process possesses its own forms of influence, which can be no less powerful than global eco-problems in deciding Europe's future; thus, they should not be overlooked by any means. If climatic changes are a plague carried through the air, the eco-domino is a fire creeping along the ground.

As we have seen in the previous chapters, the eco-domino is unlikely to stop in Russia; on the contrary, it will probably gain in speed and scale there. If present tendencies of pollution and deterioration are not reversed, and the system of environmental protection in the former USSR and the surrounding seas is not made more efficient (and there are no signs of improvement as these lines are being written), within a few years, a unified eco-domino "front," stretching from Scandinavian to Turkish borders, will be threatening Western Europe.

Yet why all this concern about Western Europe? What about the Eastern half? Has it already reached the point where it has nothing to lose? No, it is not that, but rather the problem of defining Eastern Europe in relation to Western Europe. Should it be seen as a buffer zone protecting the West from the threat of the eco-domino from the East, or as an area of its potential expansion and the intensification of its accumulated effect on the West? Evidently, it all depends on the point of view of the observer. From the standpoint of the West, Poland, Czechoslovakia, and the former East Germany—in fact, all the countries that used to form the Soviet bloc—are understood to have high levels of pollution, with damaging effects on life expectancy and the health of their populations. Indeed, this is now realized not only by Western specialists but by the general public as well: popular magazines, the news media, and *National Geographic* have shown them a landscape whose grimness defies imagination.

In Poland, 10 percent of all forests have literally withered, and a large portion has been damaged. Thirteen million Poles of a population of 40 million suffer from disorders caused by environmental pollution.[3] In Czechoslovakia, 30 percent of the forests have withered. In the worst polluted areas, up to 80 percent of the children suffer from asthma and allergies, and one-third grow up retarded.[4] Children in the industrial city of Kuklen in Bulgaria were found to have such high levels of lead in their blood that by American standards they should have been immediately hospitalized for detoxification.[5] In Silesia, children's blood contains so much lead and other heavy metals that, as early as 1984, specialists remarked that "the rate of their mental retardation was appalling."[6]

All of this is common knowledge in Russia; and yet for a Russian specialist, crossing the Polish border means moving into a different, ecologically cleaner and more stable area. This may sound strange, but in Poland most of the forests (even if weakened or dying from acid rain) are of the coniferous-deciduous type which has always existed here. By contrast, in Belarus and the area stretching up to Moscow, this indigenous type of forest has long disappeared as a result of human activity, replaced by less valuable trees such as birch and aspen. True, nearly 30 percent of Poland's population suffers from diseases caused by air, water, and soil pollution; yet Soviet figures indicate that 80 percent of all diseases are directly or indirectly related to environmental pollution.

Even the agricultural landscape in Eastern Europe looks different from that to the east; in former Soviet territories, the squares and rectangles of the fields crudely break out of the natural borders; in the former, the plots are smaller, their boundaries more in harmony with the local landscape. Soviet collective farms—and the Ministry of Land Improvement—tried to achieve better figures for field sizes by cutting down all vegetation, flattening hills, and straightening river channels, to make the land more convenient for tractors. In Poland, farmers and land-owning cooperatives leave copses, streams, and small marshes untouched; as a result, there is less erosion and damage from droughts. The Russian visitor derives pleasure even from the external appearance of Polish industrial sites and roads: there are fewer neglected, half-ruined buildings, and the roadside ditches are almost totally free of litter.[7]

So then, is the danger in the eye of the beholder? Indeed, there is some danger that the difference in perception might lead to an underestimation of the consequences of destabilization of Poland, Czechoslovakia, and neighboring countries including the former USSR. But the main cause of the danger is the deterioration and collapse of the area, and the eco-domino's advance within the immediate vicinity of Central Europe.

Cleaning Up After Communism. This phrase aptly sums up the Western attitude toward the ecological problems plaguing Eastern Europe. However, in this case brevity may border on inaccuracy. Communism is equated with something nasty and ruthless that, thank God, has come to an end. Now the Marxist slogans can be discarded along with all the rest of it, and now what is needed is more sophisticated antipollution technology. "Economic reforms and new technology may allow the centrally planned economies and the emerging democracies to develop *without* further harm to the environment," wrote the American, Soviet, and Chinese authors of an article in *Scientific American.*[8]

Establishing democracy in politics and a free market in the economy have in the past helped bring significant improvement in people's lives everywhere. I say in the past—for never before have such reforms been introduced in the context of an ecological crisis.

In Eastern Europe, political and economic reforms are proceeding more rapidly than in the countries of the former USSR, so that the conditions are more favorable for aid from the West to have a positive effect. It would appear that Eastern Europe has better chances for the future; yet even so, there has been little progress in environmental protection. Although communism has been buried, the vistas are far from cloudless, and the air is not as pure as the Western and Eastern Greens had hoped.

East Germany is the sole example of reduced pollution. Germany shut down all electric power stations using coal, outdated chemical plants, and some nuclear reactors that did not measure up to Western standards. Moreover, it cut down the transborder flow of atmospheric pollution which, to a degree, is responsible for acid rains in Poland and Czechoslovakia. But this case has nothing to teach us, since none of the other East European countries has rich relatives willing to "adopt" it regardless of cost.

Freedom and a healthy environment—these had equal weight in the eyes of many dissidents and others dissatisfied with the Communist regimes. In a sense, ecological concerns even took precedence, since on environmental issues at least some protest against the official policies was tolerated. This is what happened in Poland, Czechoslovakia, and also Bulgaria, where, in late October 1989, protests and demonstrations initiated by the Greens eventually brought about the collapse of Todor Zhivkov's regime. Alarming figures on pollution and growing rates of cancer and other dangerous diseases became a platform for all the parties and movements campaigning against the existing government.

Polish, Czech, and Hungarian dissidents had strong opinions about reducing pollution and environmental destruction, but only until they actually came to power. Once they formed new democratic governments, environmentalism ceased to be a protest against communism; now pollution became a problem that had to be solved at the expense of economic development or social benefits. With all they had achieved, these countries gained no new energy sources.

Energy should be discussed first, since virtually all of Eastern Europe uses coal as its main energy resource; what is more, it is brown coal and soft coal, otherwise known as lignite, whose combustion contributes the lion's share of pollution. Poland gets 78 percent of its energy from coal; for Czechoslovakia the figure is roughly the same, with 60 percent obtained from lignites.

Solidarity may have come to power, and Wałesa may have been elected president, but Poland must burn just as much coal for electricity and heating as it did in the past: 100 million tons per year. That means 7–8 million tons of air pollution.[9] Poland sells its high-grade coal for hard currency, while households are forced to burn lignite. Solidarity wasted no time in deleting Lenin's name from the outdated metallurgical plant at Nowa Huta, but in the name of ecology only a few of the dirtiest units were shut. "Dirty work is better than no work at all," say the steelworkers, and their view is quite understandable.

Similar reasons prevent Vaclav Havel from taking decisive measures to reorient Czechoslovakia's power industry. Environmental Protection Minister Josef Wawrocek issued a decree forbidding mothers to breast-feed their babies without passing special tests for measuring toxic levels in milk. However, replacing coal would be highly unrealistic for the present; thus, the mines in Moravia and Bohemia continue to operate, and electric power stations are belching out as much smoke as before.

Any kind of progress in improving the environment in Eastern Europe is linked to energy problems. A West German study concluded that if the amount of sulfur dioxide emitted per unit of GNP in West Germany is taken to equal 100, then the index numbers for the countries of Eastern Europe would be as follows: GDR—490, Czechoslovakia—485, Hungary—386, Poland—332, Romania—280. Today, the EC countries produce an average 62 kg of SO_2 per capita per year; while for the East European countries, despite their much lower level of production, the average output is 150 kg.[10]

Pollution is due not only to inferior fuel but also to its wasteful use. Poland, whose GNP has been estimated to be smaller than that of Belgium, uses nearly three times as much energy. If Hungary is compared with Spain, a country that is at the very bottom of the EC list for efficiency of power industry and environmental protection, the corresponding ratio is 1.6 to 1, in Spain's favor.[11]

The conclusion is obvious: there is an urgent need to shift to new technologies, in the context of a free-market economy that encourages efficient use of natural resources. One of the reasons why Poland, Czechoslovakia, and Hungary are in a hurry to convert their economies to the market system is to reduce the reckless waste of coal, oil, and electricity in every area of activity. They have become stronger believers in the free market than the most outspoken theoreticians of capitalism; Marxism has evaporated in these countries, as if it had never been their ruling ideology.

But can it be assumed that a simple conversion to a market economy will help improve the state of the environment? Energy expenditure per unit of production will probably go down, but will there be a marked decrease in pollution? This would require new energy-producing technology to replace outdated equipment throughout industry, agriculture, and the residential sector.

The easiest and cheapest way to replace coal is nuclear power. Even coal-rich Belgium produces half of its energy through atomic power stations. A few years ago, Poland, Czechoslovakia, in fact all East European countries, introduced far-reaching projects for building atomic stations. In the wake of Chernobyl, all construction was frozen, and new projects were scrapped. The nuclear reactors that Czechoslovakia and Hungary had managed to complete before the Chernobyl disaster are now functioning quite well, without breakdowns, and producing from a fourth to a sixth of the energy in those countries. Yet who would now raise his hand in favor of building new reactors, even if they are not the Chernobyl type of reactors, which had to be shut down?

Too great was the shock, and too serious the discoveries being made by Soviet and Bulgarian authorities concerning the consequences of Chernobyl, for anyone to go as far as to guarantee the safety of atomic power stations simply because the political system has changed. In 1987 a group of Serbian physicists demanded cancellation of contracts signed with Western companies for construction of atomic power stations in Yugoslavia, on the grounds that the society was ill-prepared to handle dangerous high technology. "We have not yet matured enough," they wrote, "for we lack the thousands of responsible and conscientious workers, technicians and engineers. We lack the experience, as well as efficient personnel which could be entrusted with the job of supervising atomic power stations."[12] Subsequent political events in that country seem to justify their misgivings.

Short of defining their problems as succinctly and frankly as the Serbian scientists did, all Eastern European countries clearly share their doubts. Some are more skeptical—like Poland, which puts off the development of atomic energy for the indefinite future; others less so—like Hungary, which is considering eventual purchase of new, Western-built reactors, more reliable than the old ones of Soviet manufacture.

The next alternative is hydroelectric energy. Though it has never held the high promise of nuclear power, both types of energy are now being mentioned in Eastern Europe—or rather criticized by the Greens in the same breath.

Fifteen years ago, Hungary and Czechoslovakia launched the project of building the Gabcikovo-Nagymaros hydroelectric power station on the Danube. It was 60–70 percent completed when protests by the Greens and the general public convinced the Hungarian government that the economic benefits would not justify the irreversible ecological damage. Czechoslovakia, whose share of ecological damage was much smaller, intended to continue construction of its part of the project—a dam, scheduled for completion at the end of 1992. Setting aside the political and economic aspects of the problem—now involving Austria, which has given generous loans in exchange for future energy, as well as the now separate Czech and Slovak governments—it is clear that this and any future hydroelectric power stations will not have a major impact on the energy situation. They will not result in any significant changes in the coal-based power industry of Eastern Europe.

There remain energy-saving technologies, which, though they produce no energy, permit it to be used with maximum efficiency. These technologies have been rapidly developing in Western countries, allowing them to drastically reduce energy consumption per unit of production. They are environmentally friendly and highly desirable.

However, a closer look reveals that the adoption of these technologies involves difficulties similar to those presented by nuclear technology. Qualified and reliable personnel are essential to the efficient functioning of high technology, regardless of safety problems. How many of them can be found today in countries like Poland? And how many inferior workers, incompetent by Western standards, can be brought up to par with the help of economic incentives alone?

A vicious triangle: the coal-based power industry poses the threat of an environmental disaster in the near future. Yet the two alternatives—atomic power stations and modern energy-saving technologies—raise questions about the backward state of the social environment.

Purchasing and installing of Western equipment in Polish, Czechoslovakian, Hungarian, or Romanian factories will be costly. To ensure that the purchased equipment functions at full capacity will take money and time—considerable time at that, for this involves creation of new social structures, not only to raise professional skills but also to instill the necessary work ethic.

Prior to 1989, the process of environmental deterioration throughout Eastern Europe occurred in parallel with the stagnation of the social environment. To borrow the Marxist terminology, the social infrastructure and superstructure were deteriorating simultaneously. Now these countries are undergoing marked changes in their political, social, and economic systems which make them more resistant to ecological upheavals. Still, it should be kept in mind that along with the creation of more flexible and efficient structures "at the top," destructive processes continue to endanger public health "at the bottom." There is higher social efficiency versus the further advance of the ecological disaster.

"Versus" is the key term, and time will be the decisive factor. Will these countries, particularly Poland and Czechoslovakia, have enough time to halt ecological deterioration before ecological systems collapse, either by themselves or under the pressure of the eco-domino inexorably advancing from the east? How much time do Poland, Czechoslovakia, and Romania have until they find themselves in the predicament of India's Pradesh State, which, as one of its leaders has put it, "may be well on the way to producing a subhuman kind of race where people do not have enough energy to deal with their problems"? A situation when no amount of outside help would be enough to turn back the tide; when people en masse would no longer be able to absorb technical innovations, and society would be powerless to provide them with education.

It is only natural that from the viewpoint of Eastern Europe, the model example of a stable economy and ecology is the green lawn of its neighbors the Germans, the Danes, or the Dutch. Try telling a Pole or a Czech that in "prosperous Germany," 80 percent of all the indigenous species of plants and animals may disappear within the next fifteen years. He will smile and object that in ten years 80 percent of all the Poles may disappear. There is a huge gap in perception, the difference between a pleasant and healthy environment—and an environment fit for human survival.

7

Almost a Christmas Story

On May 12, 1989, for the first time in history, a government resigned due to the failure of its environmental policy. This took place in Holland. The resignation was preceded by events that deserve a closer look.

On Christmas Day in 1988, Beatrix, Queen of Holland, broke with tradition in her regular ceremonial address to the public by discussing the acute problems facing the country. These were issues that no monarch before her had ventured to raise—namely, ecological problems. The following is an excerpt from the queen's Christmas message.

> The earth is slowly dying and the inconceivable—the end of life itself—is becoming conceivable. . . . Each generation must give new substance to the concern for nature. After a period of development and expansion—the reclamation and cultivation of the Earth—followed a period during which concern turned into exploitation. Now we are faced with a challenge of finding a new relationship with nature, characterized by respect for ecological balance, caution and careful management.[1]

Naturally, the queen had not been conducting her own research; she based her speech on a report entitled *Concern for Tomorrow,*[2] concluded a few days earlier by the Dutch Institute for Problems of Public Health and Environmental Protection. Within one day, the scientific report turned into a best-seller, with ten times as many copies sold as the publishers had expected. And the book was being read. No doubt, a speech by the queen is excellent publicity; but it is also significant that *Concern for Tomorrow* was written with insight and lucidity unmatched by any professional or "Green" publication on ecology. It combined dozens of superb diagrams and charts with brilliant analysis in which detailed research was clarified by means of clear-cut and comprehensive conclusions. "The report demonstrates that in spite of the great efforts being made and in spite of the observation that in several aspects the quality of the environment in the Netherlands has improved, a further deterioration of that quality will certainly occur if present trends persist," wrote E. Nijpels, Minister of Planning, Residential Development and the Environment, in the preface to the report.[3]

A few days after Christmas, the government decided to speed up the adoption of a long-term plan for ecological policy. Indeed, the plan had been long in the making; in fact, *Concern for Tomorrow* was written as a series of scientific recommendations for the plan. The queen's speech, and the ensuing public reaction, simply spurred and intensified the course of events.

In April the Ministry of the Environment drew up the final draft of the plan, with the expressive title "To Choose or To Lose."[4] It was at that point, in the process of finalizing the forms and deadlines for realizing the plan, that the ruling coalition was split by conflicting views. Naturally, the controversy did not center on the issues of pollution or the damage it causes. The parties clashed over the project of reducing the use of private cars by levying certain taxes. Since car owners comprise an electoral majority, none of the parties wanted to appear to be hurting the voters' interests, and the coalition broke apart. Still, this did not prevent the transition government from adopting the plan in its entirety and beginning to put it into effect, until it was continued by the new government elected in the fall of 1989.

The media supplied very scanty coverage of the entire story concerning the government's "ecological" collapse. Only the *International Herald Tribune* featured a front-page report that the

Dutch Parliament had approved a plan, unprecedented in its scale, intended to bring about radical changes in society's relation to the environment within one generation, and that by 1994 this program would be allocated $8.2 billion (the U.S. federal budget for similar objectives amounted, in 1989, to about $10 billion).

This history is one reason why I have chosen Holland as an indicator of the extent to which countries are capable of guaranteeing stability of their environment and the well-being of their citizens. The other reason is Holland's success in comparison to other countries. I am relying on the answers I received from about thirty experts in reply to my request to name the ten countries with the most efficient system of environmental protection: Holland was invariably cited among the leading five.

Among these top five countries, Holland is faced with the most complicated objective conditions. Suffice it to say out that Holland has the highest population density in the Western world. It has the highest concentration of livestock (15 million pigs, millions of cows and poultry, for a population of 15 million), and the highest density of cars per kilometer of freeways. Its shortcomings have become especially obvious in recent years, as the ecological crisis has worsened. More than half of the country lies beneath the sea level. The intricate network of canals and dams built over the centuries as a protection from the sea will prove of little avail if the level of the world ocean rises as a result of the greenhouse effect. The Rhine and the Meuse—the two large rivers in whose mouth the Netherlands are situated—bring in massive quantities of pollution accumulated throughout their basins in Germany, France, and other countries. The rivers contaminate not only the North Sea coast but also the entire network of waterways, the soil, and the ecosystems along the rivers and canals that span most of Holland. Three-quarters of the sulfurous pollutants in Holland's atmosphere have been "imported" from the neighboring countries.

Despite all this, so far Holland has managed to maintain a relatively stable environment on the whole, and there has been no

observable damage to human health due to pollution. Through
government measures, Holland's environmental budget has risen
to 3 percent of GNP (the highest share in the world), while the
number of people engaged in this sector has reached five in every
thousand inhabitants (also the highest ratio in the world)—supplemented by the recently founded environmental police. What
accounts for this success? What remains after the "dust" of im-
pressive figures on reduced air and water pollution has settled?
What political changes have taken place, and what structures
have been created?

Unfortunately, the many publications dealing with the global
aspects of ecological problems do not go into much detail in their
analysis of those factors of the market economy that go toward
alleviating ecological problems. The prosperity enjoyed by Western countries rests on the principle of free-market economy. Improvement of social conditions, including public health and
environmental protection, is a basic feature of this type of economy, a fact that is patently visible in the example of the European Community as well as other developed countries, including
Japan, Singapore, and Australia.

It took decades of social regulation and policies for the Western countries to minimize the ecological damage caused by industry, agriculture, and energy production. The basic contradiction
between the profit motive of private owners on the one hand, and
the public interest in the preservation of a healthy and aesthetic
environment on the other, still exists.

Western lawmakers realized many years ago that they could
not rely on the goodwill of individual private owners: competi-
tion means that producers with higher environmental costs are at
a disadvantage. A whole system of public regulation and law
enforcement is necessary to compel selfish individuals and companies to abide by the rules of the game. Now these rules have
become more strict and more sophisticated—not only with respect to health protection in individual shops and enterprises (for
example, in the case of lead or mercury), as was true a century

ago, but also with payment for the prevention of such long-term or long-distance damage as acid rain in adjacent areas, and liability for preservation of the ozone layer.

What are the inherent advantages of the modern market economy for maintaining environmentally friendly production? First, as a rule private enterprise is interested in the optimal utilization of natural resources and energy, and thus in reducing production costs and the waste of raw materials. Second, higher economic efficiency allows enterprises to allocate considerable funds for antipollution facilities, land reclamation, and so forth. Third, among the chief advantages of the market mechanism is its innovative capacity, which explains why the best techniques for protecting the environment have been devised within the market system.

Of course, the free market is not a magic formula or panacea. While the Western industrialized countries have achieved definite progress in environmental protection within their own borders, this does not affect, for instance, their trade policies toward the Third World countries.

Holland can serve also as a model for combining all the advantages of the market economy and overcoming national egotism. In 1989 it allocated 0.94 percent of its GNP for aid to Third World countries, second only to Norway, which contributed 1.04 percent (the figure for the United States was 0.15 percent).[5] Holland alone assigned a large share of its assistance specifically for environmental protection facilities. Only recently, Holland launched a huge forestation project in five Latin American countries, for a total area of 125,000 hectares (equal to 3.2 percent of Holland's own area). These forests will absorb as much carbon dioxide as will be emitted by Holland's coal-using electric power stations during the 1990s. Broad-mindedness is an undisputable feature of the politicians in this small country.

The projects carried out by Holland might be called "ecological missionary work." It would be difficult to find any other name for projects being put into effect in India, for instance, where it is difficult to expect the government to muster sufficient resources and means of its own to save vital resources such as water, land, and forests from total destruction.

Holland was the first West European country to embark on a policy of active cooperation with an East European country during the latter's transition to democracy. In 1989 it assisted Poland in creating the first modern automatic system for measuring pollution levels in the country's south. And it was the Dutch prime minister who introduced the idea of a European energy coalition which would assist in joining the resources of Eastern Europe and the former USSR into a unified energy system.[6]

Holland's contribution to the development of a global ecological mentality on the political level outweighs its contribution to concrete ecological projects. But we should not overlook the fact that the shaping of such a mentality requires certain structures, including a large army of qualified experts and the practical skill to implement specific policies. On what basis can such structures be developed? Under what conditions can they form a pyramid topped by political leaders who, regardless of partisanship, are committed to maintaining environmental stability and ensuring global survival?

What is the primary reason for the Dutch success? As paradoxical as it may sound, Holland's efficient handling of its ecological policies is largely due to thoughtful planning on the part of the government, which embraces all areas of management, from economy to education. This planning includes introduction of programs focused on a single objective (such as reduction of CO_2 emissions, or collection and sorting of domestic wastes for further recycling). The plans are put into effect, however, in the context of market economy, primarily through a wide range of tax benefits and subsidies.

In addition, "measures supplementing market regulations" are an important feature of every program. This includes support of new technologies and energy sources still unable to compete with others on the market; introduction of new, "maximally pollution-free" commodities; and government aid to research on human behavior and various cultures and traditions from their impact on the ecology.

In our era, when sources of pollution are controlled not only by state authorities and a finite number of manufacturers but also by the mass of consumers, the aspects of human behavior acquire a special importance. This fact is underestimated by most countries, including the Western ones. The Dutch managed to "bend" the multibranch network of ecological education to suit the mental and educational levels of various strata of the country's population, thus achieving results unmatched by any other country. The effects can be seen in the maintenance of both old and new regulations for garbage disposal as well as in the competent treatment of pollution on work sites. Writes E. Tellegen, a Dutch expert on ecological and social problems:

> On looking back, one wonders how it was possible that the nobility and the social democracy succeeded in cooperating so well for the benefit of the protection of the environment. . . . One factor which stimulated such cooperation in the Netherlands was the dominant political style in this country during the half century between 1917 and the end of the 1960s.
>
> In 1917 an accommodation was reached between conflicting religious and ideological groups. The right to found state-financed religious schools and voting rights for the working class were accepted. From that moment up to the late 1960s, Dutch society has been a "denominational" society. Parents sent their children to schools of their own religion, and even activities like raising cattle or playing soccer were organized on a denominational basis, though their leaders were used to cooperation. Indeed, "samenwerking" (cooperation) is sometimes considered by foreigners to be a typical Dutch characteristic.
>
> The Dutch style of politics enabled different ideological groups within Dutch society to cooperate with considerable success. Lijphart (1968) mentions, among other features, the following "rules of the game" in Dutch policies since 1917: (i) a businesslike attitude towards politics; (ii) the depolitization of potentially divisive issues; (iii) cooperation among different elites; and (iv) acceptance of Government decisions.[7]

As part of the Dutch pattern of cooperation, the government is accustomed to asking private organizations for advice on controversial issues. Government departments are surrounded by an "iron ring" of advisory councils through which the public can influence government decisions, thus muting conflicts.[8]

Tradition is a rather "untraditional" subject in the analysis of ecological policies, and thus it merits special attention. Certainly, traditions manifest themselves in the conduct of the Green organizations and movements. Holland has no Green party! The activities of the German Greens are widely known, and Greens are prominent in England, France, and other countries surrounding Holland. In Holland, however, the Green organizations and groups have never been represented in the Parliament—and, more importantly, have never sought representation—despite the fact that the members of the eight largest organizations alone number over 700,000 people (or about 5 percent of the country's entire population).[9] With rare exceptions, the Dutch Greens have always refrained from noisy rallies and demonstrations. They prefer, as it were, the more businesslike methods of evolution to those of revolution. Most of them are loath to engage in publicity stunts. The oldest and biggest organization, the Association for the Preservation of Natural Monuments, from the moment it was founded (1905), has been characterized by its elitist nature—from the strictly official dress code at all its rallies and meetings to the carefully regulated lexicon tolerating no unruly behavior or slang.

Yet, despite its elitist nature, it was this very association that for dozens of years managed to secure large-scale support from the general public, including influential political and financial leaders, writers, and journalists. The association's exclusivity, rather than being a drawback, played a positive role by discouraging right-wing, pro-fascist, and radical nationalist movements from exploiting the awakening "back to nature" sentiments, as has happened in other countries. In Holland, environmentalism became associated with the social-democratic youth movement. As a result, one can find among the prewar and postwar leaders of the Social Democratic party names of the same people who were active in environmental protection organizations.[10]

The budgets of all large organizations are based on direct or indirect government subsidies (sometimes up to two-thirds of their annual budget). Thus there are some grounds for skepticism as to the independence of their views on the government's environmental policy. The important issue is what happens with government subsidies. One example is the Center for Energy Saving and Clean Technology and the Center for Agriculture and Environment, founded by the eight largest environmental organizations, which provide the Greens with opportunities to monitor and criticize government policies in the areas of energy production and agriculture. The money is used for joint work with private consulting firms and scientists to analyze any problem or any project or legislation proposed by the government. In addition, every provincial and local self-governing board contains a public Green council working jointly with professional ecologists. After a series of acute conflicts caused by ecological projects and laws adopted by the government and later modified under public pressure, authorities prefer to send preliminary drafts of such projects for "approbation" to the Green organizations. This not only prevents clamorous conflicts; once they have been approved by the Greens, the projects are quickly passed by the Parliament and the local boards, and are then implemented more efficiently than before. On the whole it can be said that the tranquil relations between the Dutch public and the government are not a result of the Greens' being such "good children," but rather can be attributed to the government's sensible regard for public demands, naturally just as sensible. In addition, unlike their counterparts in other countries, the Dutch Greens are skilled in settling conflicts among themselves as well as among various groups and organizations engaged in environmental protection. The "Big Eight" forum is a good example. In the mid-1970s, scores of new environmental organizations and groups appeared on the scene, each advocating its own policy. The eight largest organizations then created a forum for permanent consultations. Once a month their leaders meet to coordinate their efforts on the national scale (assisted by a single staff secretary).[11]

On the whole, the Dutch society is marked by the rare ability to combine maximum freedom for various civil groups in their private and social activities (something that characterizes almost all Western countries) with the will and the capacity for cooperation in all vital spheres. It was this time-proven experience of cooperation among all population strata and the officials on every level, acquired in the process of creating a unique system for channeling rivers and saving the country from floods, that formed the basis that forged the country's environmental awareness faster than in other countries.

A Failure? Having described the world's most efficient national system of environmental protection, let me also note that, according to most of the experts, the bottom line of all these efforts is failure. (A characteristically Dutch detail: I heard this judgment from a high-ranking Environmental Ministry official before I heard it from the Greens.)

Natural environment has long ceased to exist in Holland, they claim. Find one wood grove in Holland that was not planted by man, one river or lake that has not been joined by canals. And they are right: there are no such woods or rivers. It is even said that there is no grass left in Holland that has not been cultivated.

What is important, however, is not the "pedigree" of Holland's landscapes and ecosystems, but rather the fact that most of the planted forests are withering due to acid rains (whose sources lie outside of Holland). Soil—the basis for the uniquely productive agriculture—is being dealt a double blow: the impact of acid rains, and that of excessive fertilization. Within the next few years they will become too saturated to absorb another drop of fertilizer. Fertilizers and pollutants are also invading the water.

The Dutch secure supplies of pure water from subterranean strata, but through what means and at what price? Liquid wastes, after a thorough, multistage process of purification and testing, are diverted to the sand dunes in the country's coastal area, where the water's natural course is to filter through the sand and replenish, drop by drop, the subterranean water level. In twenty years, according the experts, this water will hardly differ from naturally pure water. Everywhere, natural systems are replaced by artificially created and artificially maintained ones.

It would seem that the colorful plantations of Dutch flower growers only extend the natural system, or even improve it. This judgment of our eyes and aesthetic sense would pass uncontested, were it not for the scores of thousands of kilocalories of energy in the form of electricity, petrol, and other materials used for every square meter of flower greenhouses. This energy, which must be produced somewhere, destroying nature in one way or another, is then transported and burned, causing further pollution. Holland was lucky in possessing its own large stores of the purest energy source—natural gas. Furthermore, it is more efficient than any other country in utilizing methane formed in cattle wastes. Still, the share of oil and other imported energy resources is considerable.

A more cultivated landscape not only accumulates more energy as it is being created (that is in the past, and not so relevant now) but, by absorbing concentrated amounts of agricultural, industrial, and other types of output, inevitably requires enormous amounts of energy in order to keep functioning. This link, invisible yet as crucial as the umbilical cord to the embryo, must be kept in mind by anyone admiring the charming squares of Dutch fields, the well-groomed cows, and the comfortable houses (with double garages).

Therefore, if one were to draw a tentative conclusion concerning the efficiency of the Dutch system of environmental protection, it might run as follows: *The maintenance of a stable and, from the human point of view, healthy environment is feasible provided that the simplification and impoverishment of natural ecosystems is accompanied by the complication and perfection of the system of their management.* This can happen when the destruction of the society's "ground floor" is accompanied by the development of a "second floor" which exercises control over the destruction; where there is a reshifting of loads and a creation of new relations, both economic and social, even before the old ones have been destroyed.

It is easier to formulate such a conclusion than to explain what it means. Obviously, it entails the development of structures capable of rapid and flexible reaction to environmental changes—pollution, destruction, accumulating handicaps—before the damage becomes irreversible. It also includes various financial and moral incentives, and a high level of public education. Such structures cannot develop in a totalitarian society, which by its nature ignores the reverse relationship between management and the objects being managed. Yet it is the very availability and flexibility of such relationships that constitute the factor which, while not guaranteeing success, creates the possibility of success in maintaining a stable and safe environment.

In addition to the socioeconomic potential, in addition to democracy and the level of education, there is something else, something that belongs in the nebulous and undefinable sphere known as national spirit, adherence to moral tradition. If rational criteria were all that was required, other Western countries would handle environmental protection as successfully as Holland. Yet this is far from being the case, even for Holland's immediate neighbors, the Belgians, who are faring much worse. In Brussels, which has become the administrative capital of the entire European Community, to this day the framework of waste-water treatment is quite inadequate, to put it mildly, and sulfur pollution in the air exceeds all the accepted limits.[12] However, before we focus on their neighbors' shortcomings, we need to complete our analysis of the Dutch.

Failures lurked for the architects of Holland's ecological policy in two areas: private consumption and international cooperation. Let us look at international cooperation first.

Despite the many years of neighborly goodwill existing among the European nations, problems plaguing a number of countries are being dealt with at a creeping rate. The multifaceted nature of these problems too often serves as an excuse for a wait-and-see policy. "Let sleeping dogs lie" is the motto in these cases. The European Community has resisted some Dutch initiatives, including a regulation limiting the amount of cadmium in products and financial incentives to encourage the use of "clean" cars.[13] "Unfortunately," writes the former Dutch Environmental Protection Minister E. Nijpels, "international decision making is generally not known for its rapid progress."[14]

The *Concern for Tomorrow* report makes a mention of the large-scale pollution of the Meuse by salt mines and processing plants in northern France. This pollution was causing grave damage to the soil, and the Dutch farmers naturally protested. French authorities invariably objected that the amounts of salt deposited by the salt mines did not exceed the allowed norms, and that there was no international regulation determining the amount of pollution that would be safe for Dutch soil. On what grounds, therefore, should the salt-mining companies be required to spend large sums of money for additional treatment of their wastes?

This argument had a formal logic of its own. Yet the official reports did not mention that the Dutch government transferred into a Paris bank the amount required to build the treatment facilities. The French did not draw on the account. This was no longer a matter of money but rather of principle: giving preference to the ecological norms of a foreign state over those of France would create a precedent.

For a few years the money sat untouched in the bank, while the salts continued to contaminate the Dutch soil. This came to an end when an international court in the Hague examined the complaint and held that the French salt-mining companies were obliged to build the treatment facilities.

And now a couple of examples concerning private consumption.

Success in reducing pollution in industry and agriculture cannot prevent the damage accumulated over time. Even though in Holland 30 percent of commuting to work and 60 percent to school is done on bicycles, the number of cars has skyrocketed. It is on sunny summer days, when most of the population are on vacation or driving to the countryside after a workday, that the wind blowing in from continental Germany brings heavy amounts of sulfurous pollution. The share contributed by cars threatens to raise the rate of pollution to concentrations harmful to human health. Radio broadcasts appeal to the millions of Dutch to refrain from driving and use bicycles instead, or the convenient buses and trains. To no avail: the majority disregard such advice, and thus days of rest turn into days when air pollution is at its highest.

All failures are painful; yet one of them is especially unpleasant, for it concerns that part of the population which for centuries has set an example of diligence and civic virtue. They are the Dutch fishermen, who are largely Protestant. Over the last decades, fishing companies and cooperatives, with government support, have invested hundreds of millions of dollars into modernizing the fishing fleet. However, in the late 1980s the critical situation in the North Sea, indeed in the whole Atlantic Ocean, forced many governments to reduce the catch and revise the quotas. A quota was also set for the Dutch fishermen, but they deliberately challenged the law by exceeding the quota in their catch.

The ecological threat to society has remained just as urgent as it was the day Queen Beatrix gave her sensational speech. True to her principles, in her Christmas speech of 1989 the queen appealed for a reduction in consumption of energy and resources, without which it would be impossible to even slow down further degradation. She called on the people to give up the second, let alone the third family car, as well as various new gadgets encouraging chemical pollution. Next morning the Christmas tale was over: reaction to the queen's speech was disastrous. Had people tired of calls for frugality from one of the wealthiest people in Europe?

Yet the royal bungle suggests a more serious conclusion: if one of the world's most prosperous, organized, and responsible nations refuses even to consider cutting down private consumption, what other nation could be willing to do so?

8

Zones of Ecological Interest

> "*Our beliefs and customs cannot help us understand why* the bisons and wild horses have disappeared, why even the deepest forest is full of the scents of the crowd, and why the vista of rocky mountains is tangled round by a 'talking wire.' Where has the thick of the forest remained? It no longer exists. Where are the bears and the deer? They are no longer visible. Where are the eagles in the blue sky? They have disappeared. I think that this is where life ends and the struggle for survival begins."

For the bulk of the population in Western countries, life did not end with the scarcity of fauna and disappearance of beautiful landscapes, even though they did not like it. It is only today—with acid rain, with Chernobyl, with contaminated vegetables, meat, and milk, and mainly with the scarcity of basic resources, such as fresh water and fertile soil—that people are beginning to feel the narrowing of the limits of comfort and the nearing of the point of mere survival as described by the Indian chief with whose words I opened this chapter.

Holland, along with Norway and a few other nations, now finds itself in the position of the Indian chief who, far in advance of others, recognized the threat to survival. Yet, just like the Indian chief, there is little that Holland can do. "Neither our beliefs nor our traditions (nor our religions, we might add) can help us now." All of us, humankind as a whole, are creating new problems before we become aware of them, and definitely faster than we manage to find a joint means of solving them.

The lesson to be drawn from Holland's experience is, above all, that today the geography of survival—or the geography of prosperity in the case of Western countries—is ruled less by geographic factors than by the efficiency of socioeconomic structures. The key points are not proximity to the tropics or the poles, not the fast-changing climate, not the abundance or scarcity of natural resources, but society's ability simultaneously to maintain both stable economic production and the stability and safety of the environment in which it lives.

While Holland's achievements remain uniquely its own (in the sense of being hard to imitate), its main weaknesses are shared by all Western-type states, and they can help us understand to what extent these countries are capable of defending themselves against destabilization. To use a more extensive geographical analogy, today's Holland and Scandinavia may be seen as enclaves of efficient ecological policy in the midst of the rest of Europe, just as all of Western Europe is an island surrounded by deteriorating areas on virtually all sides—east, north, and south.

To be sure, today Western Europe is not faced with the environmental collapse that is plaguing Eastern Europe and the former USSR, where deterioration has begun to affect the most important resource—human beings.

While the prospect of a nuclear war remained a real threat, it was more than just a tangible obstacle to the allocation of large sums for ecological purposes. It was also an excuse for the lack of active efforts in that sphere: with the nuclear nightmare haunting the entire world, what was the point of engaging in such trifling matters? Now, when this excuse can no longer be considered serious, the West is beginning to take a realistic view of its weaknesses, and the notion of ecological safety comes to replace the nuclear obsession. The ideology of survival is becoming the ruling force in this era of dismantling the former ideological strongholds. It was probably for this reason that the linking of the threat from the East with the recognition of the weakness of ecological safety structures in most West European countries came as no surprise, least of all to the experts.

In the Cold War era, chances for survival were calculated on the basis of the balance of nuclear terror. What it meant was slow extinction for the West, a quicker demise for the East and the South. But the eco-domino process will not be stopped or even slowed down by the collapse of the Soviet empire alone.

The concept of military security of all states underwent a drastic change since the invention of intercontinental ballistic missiles. The Earth suddenly shrank in size, and distance all but lost its former defensive function. The definition of a safe and stable environment has also been completely revised with the emerging recognition of the West's dependence on the state of the environment in the East—the eco-domino effect.

"It is now clear that the situation is much worse than we though just a year ago," says Jan Fransen, an air-pollution specialist at the Dutch Environmental Institute in Utrecht. "We knew the situation in Eastern Europe was bad, but when we see it in combination with our own problems, we realize just how bad it is."[1]

The start of 1989 was marked by a noticeable rise in international activity and cooperation in the area of global ecological politics. Never before had Western and Eastern leaders expressed such concern and, more importantly, such readiness to join their efforts to protect the environment and create conditions for humankind's future survival. The number of joint bodies, as well as regulations and norms, has risen dramatically and continues to grow. Yet the question is whether all this will provide a solution to the fundamental problem of survival.

International organizations deserve credit for managing rather well their trying task; they keep up a constant flow of reports which sound such alarming notes as the following. "The average family in the Sahel requires 86 trees per year to meet its fuel wood and building needs."[2] "At the current rate of destruction, wasteland will soon surpass forests as a dominant feature of the landscape in Asia and the Pacific."[3]

Examples of the procrastination and inefficiency of international organizations are well known, even though in the area of ecology they might be more justifiable than in other spheres. I am referring to the multifaceted nature of ecological problems requiring clear-cut concepts and definitions which have to be wrapped in the crust of international laws and regulations. The chairman of the UN Legal Committee, which adopted a few years ago the agreement on a 200-mile shelf zone (a so-called zone of economic interests), said that never before had the committee been forced to spend so much time and effort in order to arrive at a geographical definition that would satisfy every side concerned. Yet what was involved here were relatively simple terms such as "shoreline" or "water area."[4] When it comes to providing clear-cut definitions for "riverbed" or "vegetation—or animal—components of an ecosystem," and fixing norms for safe levels of pollution for a number of countries with varying geographic conditions, months of debate on each of these terms appear unavoidable. A single water flow—let us speak in the language of stricter definitions—may bear varying amounts of pollution, depending on whether it passes through a rocky, sandy, or silty bed. Unfortunately, the nature of a water bed changes not only in space but in time as well—from sand to silt, for example. The diversity (spottedness) of soil cover is often such that the same forest may bear varying amounts of sulfur compounds deposited with acid rains. And what if the forest is bisected by a border? International environmental regulations are handicapped the moment they appear. This is only to be expected, since different countries will join in a concerted effort only in response to grave deterioration of natural resources, destabilization, or the danger of the total extinction of biological species. Localized dangers on a smaller scale are not considered by the UN and international organizations. This is followed by years of discussions. Even if they end in a resolution, environmental deterioration knows no recesses or breaks for seasonal holidays.

In recent years the situation has often taken irreversible turns for the worse. Here, unfortunately, the laws and norms of our civilization are in a basic conflict with Nature, particularly the nature of ecological degradation, which does not recognize such values as humanity or "a dignified level of human existence."

Since the late 1960s, the international committee that regulates whale hunting has been subjected to harsh criticism both by the scientific community and by the international press. Paul Ehrlich described this committee as an example of the inability of international organizations to take urgent action.[5] At that time the committee members justified themselves by citing the difficulties involved in estimating the size of the whale population in the ocean, and in establishing control over the whalers expected to obey the quotas. In the end, it took the extreme measures imposed by the United States and some other countries to persuade such states as Japan and Iceland—countries known not only for their wealth but also for the vast funds and efforts they invest in maintaining stability on their territories—to put a complete stop to whale hunting. The committee remains to this day a symbol of the limited effectiveness of international sanctions. Regrettably, this symbol crowns an entire pyramid of similar organizations, from the committee on the problems of desertification to the hazardous waste committee.

The creeping pace of international cooperation could be justified by citing ample reasons, both objective and subjective; but of what possible use are these justifications? No one can be blamed, but this fact should be taken into account in order to assess realistically the pace of international efforts and the level of cooperation that are called for with such urgency and genuine concern by Brundtland and other politicians as well as by such farsighted scientific organizations as the Worldwatch Institute.

There are objective factors that fundamentally contradict any serious long-term efforts to stabilize the environment, and they involve much more than the inefficiency of international organizations. Observance of international conventions and regulations costs a lot of money, and it is difficult to overcome national egotisms, which developed in a period unburdened by ecological dangers, with the possible exception of unsanitary conditions and epidemics. Egotism is always concrete, choosing to focus on tangible if minor issues in preference to graver yet presently invisible problems—in keeping with human nature. To be sure, one can hope that human nature is open to changes. This point of view is not without some basis, and there is no law against optimism. Yet even an optimist must take the time factor into account: does the rate of changes in national attitudes match the pace of ecological degradation?

In one of New Delhi's squares a board has been set up, with a new figure flashing every few seconds, indicating that another person has been added to India's population of hundreds of millions. None of the international organizations engaged in environmental protection would venture to place a similar board next to it, one that would indicate, for instance, the number of trees planted or hectares wrested back from the desert. The reason is clear: the figures would be negative. Yet if similar gauges were set up on buildings housing international ecological conferences of various sorts, this might make the public more aware of the ever-growing danger: another hectare of forests has been destroyed by acid rains; a sand desert in Kalmykia has advanced another kilometer to the west.

Indeed, the rates of environmental degradation and stabilizing measures are grossly unequal; yet in spite of this fact, or rather because of this disparity, there is no alternative to international cooperation, even though there is an obvious need to look for alternatives to the *present forms of cooperation.*

The analysis conducted in the present work demonstrates that no country can create an "island" of stability and safety from the eco-domino. Between West European countries and the environmental threat moving in from the East there are, unfortunately, no areas with ecosystems stable enough to serve as a buffer zone. On the contrary, a good portion of this territory—Silesia and Moravia, to mention two examples—is degraded to such an extent that it could accelerate the eco-domino process.

Not even Scandinavia, the most prosperous "constellation" of countries, or Japan, an island in the geographical sense, is an "island of ecological safety." From this point on, survival—dignified survival —will depend on stable surroundings, on the condition that neighboring countries, too, maintain a relatively efficient system of protection. *From now on the geography of survival will involve not only socioeconomic factors inside each country but also neighborly goodwill.* That is why the policy of cooperation and aid to weaker neighbors is a more sensible (if not the only one possible) response than attempts to construct barriers or to neutralize foreign, "imported" pollution.

This is not to say that all the experts and international organizations are unaware of their limitations and fail to look for alternative solutions. As far as the situation in East Europe is concerned, the IIASA (an international center located near Vienna, in a forest seriously damaged by acid rains) has conducted a series of studies that indicate that the West has an immediate and selfish interest in helping Eastern Europe stabilize its environment. "Helping Eastern Europe clean up its air will be the fastest and cheapest way to reduce air pollution in at least part of Western Europe," says Rod Shaw, an IIASA scientist who headed a study of the most cost-efficient ways to reduce Europe's air pollution. For every five dollars West Germany spends on cleaning acid pollutants from the atmosphere, East Europeans pointed out in 1989, it could achieve the same effect by spending one or two dollars in the East.[6] Clearly, the experts are employing the most pragmatic arguments they can find, and have made special efforts to enlist the support of international corporations.

Some EC officials are hoping to bring Japan, Canada, and the United States into the fight for better air for all of Europe. The most urgent concern is to save Europe's trees and the multibillion-dollar forest industry. Over the past two decades, the buildup of sulfur deposits and other pollutants in the soil across Europe has subjected trees in most of its forests to stunted growth, a higher susceptibility to disease, and a shorter life span.

By working to reduce Eastern Europe's pollution, Europeans will not only save money but also achieve greater success against the overall problems. In a go-it-alone approach, restoring Europe's air to a level safe for most trees would cost, at current

Map 2 **The Impact of Pollution on Europe's Forests**

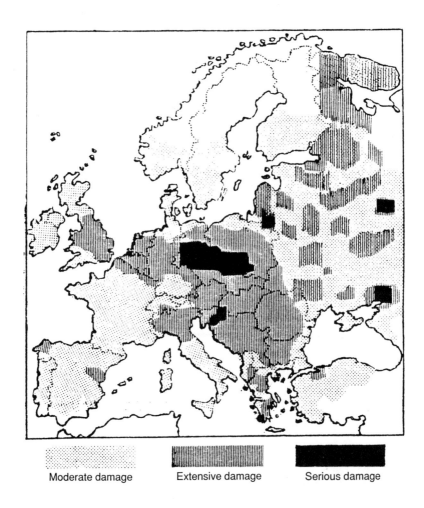

Moderate damage   Extensive damage   Serious damage

Sources: Mark M. Nelson, "Europe Confronts the Fact That Pollution, Too, Is an East-West Issue," *Wall Street Journal* (European edition), 6 February 1990; supplemented by recent Soviet data from a variety of sources.

exchange rates, a total of about $45.8 billion annually for de-
cades to come, more than six times the present spending. But that
amount could be reduced to about $16 billion per year with the
same net result if Western countries spent it in what IIASA calls
"the optimal way": diverting a large part of their environmental
budgets to East European countries to fight cross-border pollution. "Things are changing but I'm not sure they are changing
fast enough," says IIASA researcher Rod Shaw.[7]

But economic arguments do not always provide the necessary
impetus to the cause, probably because they are not the most
critical factor in forming a new ecological policy in the former
Soviet bloc. The first offers of aid to East European countries
from the West in the sphere of environmental protection cannot
be considered successful. For instance, the $50 million fund
made available to Hungary and Czechoslovakia by Scandinavian
banks for specific ecological projects was not utilized for a long
time. It turned out that the local authorities and enterprises were
incapable of rapid design and implementation of ecological projects, even when they were badly affected by pollution.

Sweden's initially extensive plans to help Poland shrank to
very humble proportions after the experts had viewed the situation from the inside. They concluded that there was little to be
done until the total replacement of all government structures
whose functions could not be taken over by foreign specialists.
Warsaw and Tirana remain the only European capitals that do not
treat their sewage, not because of difficulties involved in getting
Western aid, but because of their inability to apply it. Norwegian
and Finnish proposals for installation, under highly favorable
terms, of pollution control facilities at the two Soviet nickel
smelters in the Kola Peninsula, which export acid emissions to
Scandinavia, are being followed at a snail's pace.

During Gorbachev's visit to Norway in the spring of 1991,
there was discussion of the problem caused by the Kola emissions to all of Scandinavia; yet the Soviet leader was unable to
report any progress in respect to a joint project. "As is often the
case, a project of utmost importance . . . [for Russians] skidded to a

stop in Moscow. Now . . . it seems to have been forgotten altogether."[8]

In an agreement signed by the USSR with Finland in 1980, and with Sweden the year before, the Soviet side undertook to reduce the "export" of air pollution to these countries by 1993, by 80 percent and 40 percent, respectively. Since the Soviet side did not even make the preparations for receiving Western purification technology, these agreements were meaningless.[9] The reasons they did not make those preparations are the same I have analyzed in the preceding chapters. What rubles cannot achieve cannot always be done with dollars either, because the structures that would transform those funds into appropriate purposeful efforts are lacking.

"Common sense, i.e. pragmatism within the limits of morality, is a quality rarely found among all layers of the population, including former dissidents, present liberals, and the emerging business layer," writes a Soviet author.[10] In Russia, questions like "What is to be done?" or "Who is to blame?" still prevail over "Why should this be done? Will it be to our advantage? What will it cost?"

In order to meet the objective of providing efficient measures of ecological protection, Western assistance should embrace various spheres. In addition to financial support for projects, this assistance should include transfer of pollution-control facilities and ecological management training. However, these measures will not suffice by themselves. Assistance in a wide range of social and economic issues, directly or indirectly related to environmental protection, is also essential, in conjunction with a sound system of ecological education.

The immensity of the list of urgent problems confronting anyone involved in planning programs for Western aid to the former Soviet bloc is unprecedented not only in its geographical scope but also in the depth to which it penetrates every sphere of the life of these countries. Will the efforts and sacrifices required for this help be accepted by the Western public? Is it ready for such an involvement?

The possibilities of Western assistance are not unlimited; they should definitely be focused on concrete objectives. In my view, geographic considerations should play a crucial role here. These areas could be called "zones of ecological interest"—an analogy to the zones of economic interest established for sea-coasts. Zones of ecological interest could immediately solve a number of the problems mentioned above, by reconciling the necessity for halting the processes of global environmental degradation with the egotistical concern of every nation for its own safety above all.

The clearer are the geographic criteria for assistance, or, more simply, the closer they come to the notion of "helping a neighbor in trouble," the more likely it is that a program will enlist wide-spread public support.

In this instance, geographic factors are virtually equivalent to ecological ones. In addition to the proximity and intensity of sources of pollution, such things as climate, a common river basin, and especially landscape must be taken into account in determining which regions should be helped first. Specifically, from the point of view of West European countries, immediate and large-scale assistance aimed at halting ecological degradation should be applied first to the areas of Poland, Czechoslovakia, the Kola Peninsula, and the aquatoria of the Baltic and the Black seas. Next on the agenda should come the Baltic states, Hungary, Bulgaria, and Romania, Belarus and Ukraine and after that, some of the western parts of Russia.

It is understood that this concept of zones of ecological interest may give rise to objections on many grounds, beginning with economic and demographic and ending with purely humanitarian considerations. Counterarguments are likely to be even more numerous than those once raised against the introduction of zones of economic interest on the shelf. The real utility of zones of ecological interest is demonstrated by the fact that their shaping has already begun, without any special ideological grounds. What else if not the idea of creating a buffer zone of ecological safety would account for the projects launched by Sweden, Finland, and Norway (without much success so far) to reduce the amounts of air pollution emitted from the Kola Peninsula?

Soon after Chernobyl, Dutch specialists conducted a study of the capacity and potential danger of all the nuclear reactors located in Belgium, Germany, England, and France within the distances of 450 kilometers and 1,000 kilometers from Holland (Utrecht). Within this radius, there are at present 185 active reactors, with another 62 in various stages of construction.[11] Later a similar study was conducted by other countries. Each day brings news of increasing numbers of conferences and specific plans aimed at preventing the ecological threat emanating from sites situated in neighboring countries.

Germany and Austria have invested tens of million of dollars in ecological measures, based on the geographical criterion of proximity to the given country's border or the actual or potential source of danger. In addition, separate parts of Germany, such as Bavaria, began as early as 1988 to develop their own programs of protection against imported pollution, supplying facilities for reducing air pollution to the border areas of Czechoslovakia.[12]

Nevertheless, as important as practical measures may be, there is also an urgent need to legitimize such zones, to recognize their status as a decisive factor in the international policies of environmental protection. This is important not only in order to facilitate the lobbying of environmental programs but, above all, for the purpose of joining the efforts of various countries in strengthening and expanding their aid projects. The ecological safety interests of Western Europe or the EC countries are not limited exclusively to safeguarding the interests of Germany and Austria, as Poland and Czechoslovakia's neighbors. As demonstrated above, the long-distance effect of environmental degradation reaches much further westward—all the way to France, Switzerland, Holland, and so on. Correspondingly, there is a need to find forms of cooperation common to all of those countries.

In selected regions of limited territory, and with less limited investments, Western efforts have greater chances of stabilizing the ecological situation and slowing down the eco-domino process. Western institutions might become involved in the implementation of large-scale ecological projects, and in monitoring their effect on the environment. As a result, Western countries are bound to request participation in the decision-making process on local, regional, and even higher levels. Here the issue of national sovereignty of the western former Soviet republics—Estonia, Latvia, Lithuania, Ukraine, and Belarus—comes in with full force. At the UN Conference on Environmental Policy held in Rio de Janiero in June 1992, the newly independent states had the opportunity to discuss their ecological problems in an international forum. Ukraine, Belarus, the Baltic countries, and many others did this with great diligence. Indeed, it seemed that they hoped to strike their colleagues by the candor of their reports on the sad condition of their environment. Great was their disappointment when no one rushed to their aid with programs and funds. Yet something was accomplished at the Rio conference. It became clear to the participants that anyone who wants to influence ecological policies and practices in the former Soviet Union will have to deal with each country separately. Rio thus helped to lay the groundwork for direct contacts between Western countries and those of the old Soviet bloc. The collapse of the Soviet empire has both political and ecological implications. A process is under way in which nations are returning to their natural and historic borders. On the whole, this is a positive process in the ecological sense. An imperial totalitarian system, which disregarded in principle the importance of reverse links, has demonstrated its destructive might in its relationship with nature. It was nationalism that provided the main drive to the Green movement a few years ago—the Baltic states and Ukraine are new examples of this phenomenon—and it is capable of playing a significant role in stabilizing the ecological situation. The Baltic states and Ukraine (and, to a lesser extent, Belarus) also meet another criterion taken into consideration by Western countries in setting the scale of their aid: they clearly possess sufficiently skilled scientists and technologists, and the educational level of their populations is considerably higher than in any other part of the former empire.

At the same time, economic and social chaos, the shared basic problems of their economies, backward technology, and especially their dependence on Russia's energy—all are factors pushing these countries back into the old modes of development. In itself the new political geography of the former Soviet empire is powerless to halt environmental degradation and the eco-domino process.

However, thanks to these countries' real political independence, the idea of joining a *zone of ecological interest* may be viewed as an attractive option. This is bound to give them considerable advantages over the rest of the Commonwealth of Independent States. Even though any partnership between these countries and the West must be modeled on a different pattern than, for example, the cooperation among the EC states (there is too large a gap between their contributions and management experience), this option may prove highly profitable for both sides. For the West this may provide ways to slow down environmental degradation, while the Baltic states, Ukraine, and Belarus will have the chance to embark on a more realistic path toward dignified coexistence (if not survival itself) under conditions of a continuing global ecological crisis.

It only remains to conclude that the zone concept, while offering solutions for immediate problems, does not deal with the East—the enormous areas in Russia's North and in Central Asia that constitute the epicenters and the moving force behind the eco-domino. The main danger of destabilization remains, and it is still conceivable that the unified "front" from the Kola Peninsula to the Black Sea, which can be fought through zones of ecological interest, will refuse to act like a military front by sticking to frontal, head-on attacks.

The process under way in Central Asia has clear potential to join the accelerating desertification and environmental degradation in Iran and Pakistan. Similar tendencies are in evidence not only in the area of ecological structures but also in politics, opening the possibility of new Khomeini or Saddam types of regimes in Uzbekistan, Turkmenia, and Tajikistan. This convergence is happening against the backdrop of progressive depletion of basic natural resources (soil and water) involving the entire region.

According to experts at the Max Planck Institute in Hamburg, the ecological disaster in the Persian Gulf area, triggered by the smog caused by hundreds of burning oil wells, serves as a catalyst for environmental degradation throughout the region. This factor will have a long-term destabilizing effect, regardless of political developments in the Persian Gulf. Then a grave blow will threaten the Mediterranean coast of Europe—Greece, the former Yugoslav republics, Italy—countries that are not well equipped to preserve the stability of their environment even without outside impact.

"Whenever attempts are made to find a remedy for the ecological catastrophe in the USA or Sweden," writes Soviet biologist and Green activist S. Zabelin,

> I think of Turkmenia. There the living environment is shrinking before your very eyes, like shagreen leather, while the remedy for the high mortality rate is supplied by the high birth rate. But the majority of the Asian population, indeed the majority of today's mankind, are much closer to the residents of Turkmenia than of the United States. The future, accordingly, should be forecast while standing on the shore of the Aral Sea, not Lake Michigan. And the shore of what used to be the Aral reveals a horrifyingly alarming picture.[13]

Indeed, looking at the Aral one can see the growing expanse of the Sahara, the deserts of Namibia and the Gobi, of South America and Mexico, the tundra of the Russian North, and the slower growing ones of Canada and Alaska. These are the centers of global environmental degradation, and they will determine, within the near future, the geography of survival of our civilization. Which part of it will manage to preserve sufficient stability by "hiding" behind less fortunate neighbors? Which of the latter will grasp the opportunity for neighborly relations with stable developed countries, and which will continue to deteriorate, closing the gap between their natural resources and overpopulation with the help of epidemics and wars?

Notes

Chapter 1

1. Paul R. Ehrlich, "World Population: A Battle Lost?" *Stanford Today*, Winter 1968.
2. Quoted in Barry Commoner, *The Closing Circle: Nature, Man, Technology* (New York, 1971), p. 3.
3. *Time*, vol. 33, no. 1 (1989), p. 33.

Chapter 2

1. M. Lemeshev, "Razrushitel'naia postup' uskoreniia," *Ekologicheskaia al'ternativa* (Moscow: Progress, 1990), p. 207.
2. A. Iablokov, "Sostoianie okruzhaiushchei sredy v SSSR v 1988," *Environmental Policy Review*, vol. 4, no. 1 (January 1990), p. 6.
3. V. Larin, "Aral . . . Baikal . . . Iamal . . . ?" *Strana i mir*, 1990, no. 2, p. 79.
4. B. Kochurov et al., "Osnovnoe soderzhanie karty ostrykh ekologicheskikh situatsii," *Prirodno-ekologicheskie sistemy* (Moscow: Moscow Section of the Geographical Society, 1989), pp. 30–41.
5. N. Reimers and F. Shtilmark, *Osobo okhraniaemye prirodnye territorii* (Moscow, 1978), p. 157.
6. "Zabolevshee nebo," *Moskovskie novosti*, 3 September 1989, p. 18.
7. Iu. Golubchikov, *Ustoichivost' severnykh ekosistem k antropogennomu vozdeistviiu*, Seriia "Znanie" RSFSR (Moscow, 1990), p. 5.
8. Larin, "Aral . . ."
9. Ibid, p. 81.
10. Golubchikov, *Ustoichivost'*.
11. A. Iablokov, "Sel'skoe khoziaistvo bez pestitsidov," *Ekologicheskaia al'ternativa* (Moscow, 1990), p. 511.
12. Z. Wolfson, "The Environmental Risk of the Developing Oil and Gas Industry in Western Siberia," *Siberia 1*, Siberian Questions, Institut d'Etudes Slaves (Paris, 1985), p. 185.
13. Iu. Golubchikov and Iu. Solomatin, "Metodicheskie aspekty ustoichivosti severnykh ekosistem," *Issledovanie ustoichivosti geosistem*

severa (Moscow: Moscow State University, 1988), pp. 20–26.
  14. V. Kriuchkov, *Chutkaia sabarktika* (Moscow: Nauka, 1976), p. 23.
  15. Iablokov, "Sostoianie," pp. 6, 10.
  16. V. Katasonov, "Ugroza ekologicheskogo kolonnializma," *Ekos,* January 1991, p. 31.
  17. Kochurov, "Osnovnoe soderzhanie," p. 34.
  18. Golubchikov, *Ustoichivost'*, pp. 5, 6.

Chapter 3

  1. *Pravda Vostoka,* 3 September 1989, p. 3.
  2. K. Chagylov, "Vkus vody," *Turkmenskaia iskra,* 20 April 1988, p. 2.
  3. V. Seliunin, "Aral'skaia katastrofa," *Novyi mir,* 1989, no. 5, p. 237.
  4. *Pravda Vostoka,* 4 March 1989, p. 2.
  5. Seliunin, "Aral'skaia katastrofa," pp. 236, 237.
  6. *Moskovskie novosti,* 8 April 1990, p. 4.
  7. "Sredniaia Aziia i Kazakhstan: prioritety i al'ternativy razvitiia," *Kommunist,* 1989, no. 15, p. 37.
  8. "Desant," *Sem'ia,* 1989, no. 40, p. 8.
  9. A. Iablokov, "Pestitsidy, ekologiia, sel'skoe khosiaistvo," *Kommunist,* 1988, no. 15, pp. 35, 36.
  10. A. Avdeev and I. Troitskaia, "Demograficheskii aspekt razvitiia ekonomiki na rubezhe XXI veka," *Planovoe khoziaistvo,* 1990, no. 12, p. 70.
  11. Incidentally, a book by Patricia Carley recently published in England is entitled just that—*The Price of the Plan.* See C. Tuler, "Worse than Chernobyl," *Financial Times,* 29 July 1989, p. 11 (Weekend FT).
  12. The estimate is based on figures from the following articles: B. Ataniiazov, "Razvitie vodosberegaiushchikh tekhnologii proizvodstva," *Voprosy ekonomiki,* 1988, no. 6, pp. 121, 122; N. Minashina, "Soizmeriaia dokhody i poteri," *Nash sovremennik,* 1987, no. 1, p. 125. Also "Profitability of Cotton Growing in 1871–72," Institute of Farm Income Research, September 1973, Tel Aviv (Hebrew); reprinted in *Selected Papers. Israel Environmental Protection Service,* 1978, no. 6, p. 45 (English).
  13. Ataniiazov, "Razvitie," p. 122.
  14. M. Agursky, Hebrew University, personal communication, summer 1990.
  15. *Literaturnaia gazeta,* 11 August 1989, p. 3.
  16. *Literaturnaia gazeta,* 29 January 1989, p. 10.
  17. *Pravda Vostoka,* 1 August 1989, p. 3.
  18. Ibid.
  19. *Komsomolets Turkmenistana,* 20 April 1989, p. 2.
  20. *Literaturnaia gazeta,* 27 January 1988, p. 12. Also *Izvestiia,* 28 February 1987, Interview with the Chairman of the Council of Ministers of Uzbekistan, S. Sultanova.
  21. S. Poliakov, "Ostavit' Sredniuiu Aziiu v pokoe," *Strana i mir,* 1990, no. 4, pp. 125–27.
  22. "Sredniaia Aziia i Kazakhstan," p. 37.

23. I. Bogdanov, "Uchit'sia pravde," *Zvezda Vostoka* (Tashkent), 1988, no. 5, p. 44.
24. A. Monin, "Zastoinye zony," *Novyi mir*, 1988, no. 7, p. 165.
25. "Sredniaia Aziia i Kazakhstan," p. 33.
26. Z. Wolfson, "The Central Asia Environment: A Dead End," *Environmental Policy Review*, vol. 4, no. 1 (1990), p. 42.
27. I. Zabelin, "Liudi, kotorym ne vse ravno," *Spasenie*, 1991, no. 3 (April), p. 3.

Chapter 4

1. V. Seliunin, "Aral'skaia katastrofa," *Novyi mir*, 1989, no. 5, p. 235.
2. Ibid., p. 209.
3. Alan B. Durning, "Mobilizing at the Grassroots," *State of the World* (1989), p. 168.
4. Seliunin, "Aral'skaia katastrofa," p. 209.
5. Reuters, 2 June 1990.
6. Z. Wolfson, "The Caspian Sea: Clear Signs of Disaster," *Environmental Policy Review*, vol. 4, no. 2 (1990), pp. 16, 17.
7. Ibid., p. 15.
8. A. Monin, "Zastoinye zony," *Novyi mir*, 1988, no. 7, pp. 162, 163.
9. B. Ermolaev, "Gazovaia ataka," *Energiia*, 1990, no. 7, p. 13.
10. *Kazakhstanskaia pravda*, 2 February 1989, p. 1.
11. A. Iablokov, "Sostoianie okruzhaiushchei sredy v SSSR v 1988," *Environmental Policy Review*, vol. 4, no. 1 (1990), p. 5. Also B. Vinogradov, "Aerokosmicheskaia ekspertiza v knige," *Ekologicheskaia al'ternativa* (Moscow: Progress, 1990), p. 561; D. Kugul'dinov, "The Kalmyk Steppe Cries Out for Help," *Ecos*, January 1990, pp. 18–21.
12. Vinogradov, "Aerokosmicheskaia ekspertiza," p. 558.
13. S. Konovalov, "Volga: ekologicheksii diagnoz," *Ekologicheskaia al'ternativa* (Moscow: Progress, 1990), p. 240.
14. Iablokov, "Sostoianie," p. 2.
15. *Financial Times*, 14 December 1990, p. 2.
16. Iablokov, "Sostoianie," pp. 7, 8.
17. *Spasenie*, 3 April 1991, p. 3.
18. Z. Wolfson, "The Central Asia Environment: A Dead End," *Environmental Policy Review*, vol. 4, no. 1 (1990), pp. 37–39.

Chapter 5

1. Hilary E. French, "Green Revolution: Environmental Reconstruction in Eastern Europe and the Soviet Union," Worldwatch, Paper 99 (November 1990), p. 5.
2. A. Iablokov, "Sostoianie okruzhaiushchei sredy v SSSR v 1988," *Environmental Policy Review*, vol. 4, no. 1 (1990), pp. 1–11.

3. M. Lemeshev, "Razrushitel'naia postup' uskoreniia," *Ekologicheskaia al'ternativa* (Moscow: Progress, 1990), p. 201.

4. Ibid., p. 205.

5. V. Andreev, "Poka ne pozdno," *Izvestiia,* 6 February 1990, p. 3.

6. The data are drawn, respectively, from M. Lemeshev, *Ecologicheskaia al'ternativa* (Moscow: Progress, 1990), p. 205; N. Vorontsov, from an inteview on Moscow television on 16 April 1990; N. Reimers, in *Trud,* 26 February 1991, p. 2; and T. Ivanov and N. Glovatskii, in *Planovoe khoziaistvo,* 1990, no. 7, p. 108, where the same authors estimate the budget necessary to create "conditions for a healthy living" at 1,000 billion rubles.

7. F. Morgun, "Ekologiia v sisteme planirovaniia," *Planovoe khoziaistvo,* 1989, no. 2, p. 61. Also B. Khorev, "Economic Decentralization and Regionalism," *Izvestiia vsesoiuznogo geograficheskogo obshchestva,* 1990, no. 2.

8. *Sovetskaia Rossiia,* 5 April 1990, p. 2.

9. Report by Academician N. Bogomolov at the conference "The Economy of Eastern Europe During Transition to a Free Market," held at Hebrew University, 9–14 April 1991.

10. A. Perlovsky, "Budget to Fight Pollution in Poland 1980–1985," *Environmental Policy Review,* vol. 1, no. 1 (1987), pp. 38, 39.

11. Andreev, "Poka ne pozdno."

12. *Sovetskaia Rossia,* 20 January 1989, p. 2.

13. I. Bashmakov and A. Makarov, "Slol'ko mozhno nachiniat' 'bombu'?" *Energiia,* 1990, no. 7, pp. 23, 24.

14. Ibid., p. 25.

15. B. Bushuev, chairman of the Energy Subcommittee of the USSR Supreme Soviet, "Tri kita zhizni," *Pravda,* 24 December 1990, p. 3.

16. Ibid.

17. Ibid.

18. *Pravda,* 15 February 1991, p. 2.

19. M. Lemeshev, "A Life-and-Death Conflict," *Ekos,* 1990, no. 1 (January), p. 16.

20. V. Iaroshenko, "Partii interesov," *Ekologicheskaia al'ternativa* (Moscow: Progress, 1990), pp. 77–79.

21. S. Zabelin, "Liudi, kotorym ne vsio ravno," *Spasenie,* 1991, no. 3 (April), p. 3.

22. Lemeshev, "Razrushitel'naia postup'," p. 204.

23. V. Kochurov at al., "Osnovnoe soderzhanie karty ostrykh ekologicheskikh situatsii," *Prirodno-ekologicheskie sistemy* (Moscow: Moscow Section of the Geographic Society, 1989), pp. 30–41.

24. V. Kotliakov, "Znaki bedy," *Smena,* 1989, no. 12, p. 73.

25. *Izvestiia,* 26 March 1990, p. 3.

26. Iu. Scherbak's report at the conference "Environmental Problems and National Tensions in the USSR" held at Hebrew University 2–4 January 1990. The theses were published in *Environmental Policy Review,* vol. 4, no. 1 (1990), pp. 17, 18.

27. *Kievskaia pravda,* 24 April 1991.

28. *Rabochaia gazeta,* 23 March 1991.

29. Iablokov, "Sostoianie," p. 14.

30. G. Sidorenko and V. Krut'ko, "Sokhranit' zdorov'e natsii," *Ekologicheskaia al'ternativa* (Moscow: Progress, 1990), pp. 775, 776.

31. Interview with Professor D. Sokolov, *Energiia,* 1990, no. 10, p. 19.

32. I. Altshuler, Presentation at the Harrogate Congress for Soviet and East European Studies, 25 July 1990.

33. *Izvestiia,* 31 August 1989, p. 2; *Trud,* 14 June 1989, p. 4.

34. M. Sobelman, "The Ecological Tragedy of Upper Silesia," *Environmental Policy Review,* vol. 3, no. 2, p. 31.

35. G. Batsanova, "Za zhivoi vodoi," *Pravda,* 15 March 1990, p. 2.

36. M. Bogdanov and O. Khoperskaia, "Degradatsiia i gibel' stada russkogo oserta," *Ekologicheskaia al'ternativa* (Moscow: Progress, 1990), pp. 263, 264.

37. *Pravda vostoka,* 4 March 1989, p. 3.

38. K. Gofman, professor of economics, "Gde vziat' milliardy chtoby spasti prirodu?" *Izvestiia,* 8 January 1991, p. 2. Also Iablokov, "Sostoianie," pp. 12, 13.

39. Iu. Tepliakov, "Eshchio dyshish', Ural?" *Moskovskie novosti,* 24 March 1990, pp. 8, 9.

40. *Pravda,* 26 March 1991, p. 3.

41. N. Amosov, "Kak zhit' chtoby vyzhit'?" *Literaturnaia gazeta,* 18 July 1990, p. 12.

42. S. Zabelin, personal report, March 1990.

43. The weekly *Sem'ia,* 1989, no. 49, p. 16.

44. Kotliakov, "Znaki bedy," p. 77.

Chapter 6

1. G. Iavlinskii et al., "Plius 'bol'shaia semiorka'," *Pravda,* 20 May 1991, p. 3.

2. W. Stigliani et al., "Future Environment for Europe," IIASA *Executive Report* (Austria), no. 15 (February 1989).

3. S. Golubchikov, "Chelovek protiv sebia," *Energiia,* 1990, no. 10, p. 23.

4. V. Sobell, "The Systemic Roots of the East European Environmental Crisis," *Environmental Policy Review,* vol. 4, no. 1 (1990), p. 48. Also "Clearing Up After Communism," *The Economist,* 17 February 1990.

5. Hilary E. French, "Green Revolution: Environmental Reconstruction in Eastern Europe and the Soviet Union," Worldwatch Paper 99 (November 1990), p. 23.

6. Ibid., p. 24.

7. Golubchikov, "Chelovek protiv sebia," p. 24.

8. W. Chandler, A. Makarov, and Zhou Dadi, "Energy for the Soviet Union, Eastern Europe and China," *Scientific American,* September 1990.

9. "Clearing Up After Communism."

10. J. Slama, "An International Comparison of Sulphur Dioxide Emissions," *Journal of Comparative Economics,* no. 10 (1986), p. 24.

11. "Clearing Up After Communism."

12. V. Zaharescu, "The Echo of Chernobyl in Yugoslavia," *Environmental Policy Review,* vol. 2, no. 1 (1988), pp. 33, 34.

Chapter 7

1. Quoted from "To Choose or To Lose," National Environmental Policy Plan, Second Chamber, sessions 1988–1989, the Netherlands.

2. *Concern for Tomorrow. A National Environmental Survey, 1985–2010,* 1989. The Dutch edition appeared at the end of 1988.

3. Ibid., p. vii.

4. "To Choose or To Lose."

5. S. Postel and C. Flavin, "Reshaping the Global Economy," *State of the World,* 1991, p. 173.

6. *Izvestiia,* 21 June 1991, p. 5.

7. E. Tellegen, "The Environmental Movement in the Netherlands," *Progress in Resource Management and Environmental Planning,* vol. 3, 1981, pp. 7–8.

8. J. Frouws and E. Tellegen, "The Place of the Environment in Political Strategies and Argument," p. 10.

9. Ibid., p. 8.

10. Ibid., p. 5.

11. "The Environmental Movement in the Netherlands," p. 11.

12. Tellegen, "Europe Confronts the Fact That Pollution, Too, Is an East-West Issue," *Wall Street Journal* (European edition), 6 February 1990.

13. Frouws and Tellegen, "The Place of the Environment," p. 4.

14. E.H.T.M. Nijpels, preface to *Concern for Tomorrow,* p. vii.

Chapter 8

1. "Europe Confronts the Fact That Pollution, Too, Is an East-West Issue," *Wall Street Journal* (European edition), 6 February 1990.

2. U.N. High Commission on Refugees, *Worldwatch,* vol. 4, no. 4 (1991), p. 6.

3. Ibid., U.N. Economic and Social Commission for Asia and the Pacific.

4. Prof. Janusz Symonidis, UN officer, personal communication, summer 1989.

5. Paul R. Ehrlich, "World Population: A Battle Lost?" *Stanford Today,* winter 1968, series 1, no. 22.

6. "Europe Confronts."

7. Ibid.

8. *Pravda,* 5 June 1991, p. 4.

9. Background Brief, Foreign and Commonwealth Office, London, October 1989, p. 4.

10. O. Iuriev, "Mesto otsutstviia," *Strana i mir*, no. 4, p. 132.

11. *Concern for Tomorrow. A National Environmental Survey, 1985–2010*, 1989, p. 107.

12. Background Brief, p. 6.

13. S. Zabelin, "Liudi kotorym ne vse ravno ... Spasenie," *Ekologicheskaia gazeta*, 1991, no. 3 (April), p. 3.

Index

About the Author

Ze'ev Wolfson was born in Russia in 1944. He is the author of the book *The Destruction of Nature in the Soviet Union*, a pathbreaking account of the ecological disasters in the Communist bloc which appeared under the pseudonym Boris Komarov. Widely circulated in *samizdat* and in numerous Western editions, the book attracted considerable attention—including that of Andrei Sakharov—and was awarded the Gambrinus Prize in 1983. This acclaim occasioned speculation about the author's identity, which did not become known until he emigrated to Israel in the 1980s. Wolfson is now affiliated with the Mayrock Center for Russian and East European Research at the Hebrew University of Jerusalem where he is editor-in-chief of *Environmental Policy Review* (*The CIS and Eastern Europe*).